PIRATES & ROGUES
of Monterey Bay

D1738591

PIRATES & ROGUES

of **Monterey Bay**

Todd Cook

THE
History
PRESS

Published by The History Press
Charleston, SC
www.historypress.com

Copyright © 2019 by Todd Cook
All rights reserved

First published 2019

Manufactured in the United States

ISBN 9781467143639

Library of Congress Control Number: 2019947289

Notice: The information in this book is true and complete to the best of our knowledge. It is offered without guarantee on the part of the author or The History Press. The author and The History Press disclaim all liability in connection with the use of this book.

All rights reserved. No part of this book may be reproduced or transmitted in any form whatsoever without prior written permission from the publisher except in the case of brief quotations embodied in critical articles and reviews.

This book is dedicated to Mom and Dad, who encouraged me along the book-writing path, and to my lovely wife, Elsie, who is always there to support me and be my first go-to for help when I'm baffled by new technology.

Contents

Acknowledgements

Were it not for the many excellent books by Randall Reinstedt on the history of Monterey Bay, Monterey County and the state of California, this book would not exist. Reinstedt's works were undoubtedly what piqued my interest in the fascinating history of Monterey Bay in the first place.

I would also like to give a special thanks to Mr. Don Vanderpluym, who gave the "OK" to share the Spanish coin of his late father, Garland Vanderpluym, and to Tom Tanner, who facilitated communication and provided some key historical information that can be found herein.

Picturesque Mission Ranch Meadows, beyond which Carmel River Beach, the possible scene of early 1700s pirate-related activity, can be seen. *From author's photo collection.*

Introduction

The Monterey Peninsula, a misty, pine tree–covered stretch of California's Central Coast, is known for several things: incredibly beautiful scenery along its shores, golf courses that are world-class caliber and world-class picturesque, a federally designated marine preserve, one of the nation's most celebrated aquariums, enchanting seaside hamlets like Pacific Grove and Carmel-by-the-Sea and for being the former stomping grounds of prize-winning author John Steinbeck and the setting of some of his most famous works, such as *Cannery Row* and *Tortilla Flat*.

The Monterey Peninsula is also known for its history, of which it has *a lot*, and that is putting it mildly. In fact, one writer said that virtually every major event in the first sixty years of California's existence either began or ended on the Monterey Peninsula. That assertion is hard to counter—after all, prior to its annexation by the United States, the Monterey Peninsula was the Spanish and Mexican capital of Alta (Upper) California. In fact, Monterey Bay was not only the secular capital of the California Territory for most of the pre–United States period from 1770 to 1846, but it was the religious capital as well (the Carmel Mission was usually the headquarters from which the padre-presidenté would oversee the missions of Alta California). There is much more to Monterey Bay's fascinating history than what can be seen today, preserved above ground: the weathered Spanish missions and churches, the quaint white-walled and red tile–roofed adobes of the Spanish and early Mexican periods and the two-story-tall, balconied New England–style government buildings of the late Mexican and early United States periods (these aged structures are favorite stops along Monterey's "Path of History" Walking Tour). Not as evident are remnants of California's Native history, though there are several sites that exist on the Monterey Peninsula. Historians have identified village sites that date back several centuries, to a time before the first Spanish explorers had arrived. Jumping ahead several centuries in Monterey's history, the area witnessed significant history during the Gold Rush period: the creation and signing of California's first constitution in 1850, the era of bustling Chinatowns and Chinese fishing villages from the mid-1800s through the early 1900s, the history of the Gilded Age coming of the luxurious Hotel Del Monte in 1880, a flourishing early twentieth-century artists' and writers' colony in Carmel and the gritty Monterey fishing industry period that was made famous by Steinbeck's novel *Cannery Row*. Be assured, this is only a short list of the history that can be found on the Monterey Peninsula.

Amid all this history, however, a certain chapter of the story of the Monterey Peninsula tends to be overlooked. Perhaps this is because, with one notable exception, traces of this particular chapter have all but vanished. Yet, it did happen, right here on the shores of Monterey Bay. I'm talking about Monterey Bay's pirate history!

Now, many locals will tell you, "Of course Monterey Bay has pirate history." They will then proceed to tell you about the 1818 Hippolyte Bouchard attack on Monterey. Well, they are correct to bring up this attack, and, indeed, this event constitutes a major section in this book. In fact, here is a tiny preview of that chapter: To begin with, if you have ever had the pleasure of stepping on board the *Pirates of the Caribbean* boat ride at either Disneyland or Disney World, you will remember the part where your boat passes between a coastal fort and a pirate ship in the harbor. The fort and the pirate ship trade cannon volleys while you watch, without the slightest thought to your safety! There are loud bursts of cannon fire, the whistles of cannon balls fly over your head and the water around you splashes startlingly as errant artillery falls short of its target. Well, something a lot like that actually happened in Monterey during the attack of 1818. And the part of the ride where the pirates run amok as they pillage the burning Spanish town they have sacked? That also happened during that 1818 attack on Monterey! I'm starting to get a bit ahead of my story, so I will stop there for now.

Getting back to the generalities of Monterey Bay pirate history, what many local Monterey area historians may not even realize is that there is a good deal more to Monterey Bay pirate history than just that one traumatic event. In fact, from my years of studying the history of Monterey Bay, it has occurred to me that when the pirate-related history of the peninsula is tallied up, Monterey Bay clearly deserves the title of "Pirate Central" for not only the California coast but for the entire Pacific Coast of the United States! Granted, the Santa Barbara area can put up a respectable challenge, but the scope of pirate history on that stretch of the California coast simply does not match that of Monterey Bay. It is my hope that after reading this guidebook, you will see why that is.

Now there are multiple ways to organize a guidebook on Monterey Peninsula's pirate history. One way would be to discuss each site in "road" order. In other words, one could lay out a general Monterey Peninsula pirate history tour road route and discuss each site as if the reader were visiting them. The disadvantage of writing a book in this way would be that the pirate history—as you read about it—would be jumping all over the place. It would be kind of like a movie with annoying flashbacks and flash-forwards interrupting the flow of the story. And that's not good, is it?

Instead, I have elected to lay out the chapters of pirate history in chronological order. That is, with one glaring exception: the first chapter. The first stops on this pirate tour actually examine the most recent pirate event of Monterey Peninsula's history. This was done for a reason—mainly so that the book could close with the climactic 1818 Bouchard attack. In doing this, not only would the book end on a more dramatic note, but (with the first chapter excepted) the rest of the pirate history would also fall neatly into chronological order.

Lastly, even though tales and rumors of pirate treasure are often deemed essential to any pirate-related work, this guidebook will not be pointing you in the direction of any potential buried pirate treasure. Why? Because if I knew of any such treasure, I would be out looking for it myself instead of writing a pirate history book! Okay, in all seriousness, I will simply confess that I do not know of any buried pirate treasure on the Monterey Peninsula. There *are*, however, several stories that tell of buried treasure on the Monterey Peninsula, but they are generally connected to nineteenth-century American outlaws, Mexican banditos, Gold Rush–period feuds, etc., not pirates. And, by the way, for anyone who is interested in such buried treasure lore, I recommend they read the thoroughly enjoyable books of local historian and writer Randall Reinstedt. This is not to say that the pirates who set foot on the Monterey Peninsula neglected to leave anything behind but that any artifacts that have been found thus far, while they are certainly valuable in a local history sense, hardly constitute monetarily valuable "treasure." As a final word on the subject of pirate treasure: even though I

A 1678 engraving of notorious pirate Bartholomeus de Portugees. *Courtesy of the Library of Congress Prints and Photographs Division.*

don't know of any specific tales of buried pirate treasure in Monterey, such a possibility can never be ruled out. New historical discoveries are found all the time. For instance, did you know that the *Queen Anne's Revenge*, the flagship of the notorious pirate Blackbeard, has recently been found in the waters off North Carolina? To that end, who knows what may one day come out of the sands and waters of the Monterey Peninsula.

A General Background on Pirates

Pirates have been around for thousands of years, and pirates are still active in parts of the world today. In short, piracy has never been completely eradicated from the face of the earth. However, there was a period when pirates and piracy were an ever-present scourge on the high seas—a period that often brings to mind figures, images and scenes from books and movies like *Treasure Island* and *Pirates of the Caribbean*. While these are works of fiction, they are based on a very non-fictional period of history. There really was an "Age of Pirates," the absolute peak of which would have occurred between 1650 and 1720. This was a time when terrifying scoundrels of the sea prowled the waters of the Caribbean and Atlantic oceans in wooden ships that flew black flags with skeletal designs, hunting for ships that may have been carrying a cargo of valuables. While characters like Long John Silver or Captain Jack Sparrow are fictional, terrifying pirates like Sir Henry Morgan and Blackbeard were most certainly not!

While the peak of the overall Age of Pirates took place approximately between 1650 and 1720, the general era actually began several decades before 1650 and lasted just beyond the 1720s. The Age of Pirates arguably began with swashbuckling Elizabethan-period British pirates, such as Sir Francis Drake, Thomas Cavendish and John Hawkins. These men were aggressive sea captains who preyed on Spanish treasure galleons sailing through the waters of the Caribbean and Pacific Oceans on their way back to Spain and the Spanish New World. These Elizabethan period sea mercenaries—known at the time as "privateers" (a privateer being a more

This page: These seventeenth- and eighteenth-century book illustrations depict the mayhem and terror wrought by pirates, not only on the high seas but also in enemy harbors and on land as well. *Courtesy of the Library of Congress Rare Books Division.*

respectable, officially sanctioned pirate)—also attacked Spanish coastal towns under the guise of the English flag (England and Spain were then wartime foes). Later, French and Dutch pirates also joined in on the (sometimes) lucrative endeavor of piracy on the high seas. These men mostly committed their acts of piracy in the Caribbean and Atlantic Oceans, for it was in these two bodies of water that most of the Spanish treasure ship "action" was taking place. These pirates knew that the holds of Spanish galleons were typically laden with coined silver and gold mined in the New World—in places like the ore-filled mountains of Mexico, Bolivia and Peru.

This phenomenon of pirates preying on Spanish treasure ships began in the late 1500s and continued until the 1730s. Then, when colonization in the New World began to expand beyond the Spanish settlements in Latin America (the British, Dutch and French were colonizing the Atlantic Coast of America and Canada throughout the 1600s and into the 1700s), piracy started to affect not just the Spanish but other European nations as well. Expanding colonization meant more merchant ships were carrying valuables across the Atlantic and Caribbean Oceans, thus, there were more ships for pirates to rob!

Piracy was finally brought under control around the 1730s, though it never completely died out. In fact, a second, but less spectacular Age of Pirates sprung up again in the early 1800s. This period witnessed the scourge of the Barbary pirates in the Mediterranean Ocean, as well as the problem of British pirates kidnapping Americans to be impressed into service on British vessels. The noted French pirate and privateer Jean Lafitte was also active in the Gulf Coast region of the United States during the War of 1812. And, as mentioned previously, there were the attacks of privateer Hippolyte Bouchard on Spanish California strongholds in 1818.

So, which nations produced pirates, and which nations did those pirates victimize? Well, let's start off with generalities and gradually move toward specifics. The waters just off the eastern shores of the New World (North and South America) were the primary theater for pirate activity, particularly in the first part of the Age of Pirates (1570 to 1730). Again, pirates were active in that region because, at that time, most of the world's gold and silver was being mined in Spanish Latin America, loaded onto ships—usually Spanish ships, sometimes Portuguese—and sailed either across the Caribbean or Atlantic Ocean to Spain for the purpose of filling up the coffers of the Spanish king. Spanish gold and silver was also being sailed across the Pacific Ocean at this time to be used to purchase goods in Asia. This all meant that the usual victims of piracy were the Spanish—because they controlled most of the New World territories from which the gold and silver was mined! At least that's how it played out in the beginning. In later years, *any* ship from *any* nation that held territories in the New World that also happened to be carrying valuables was a prime target for pirate attack and robbery. In other words, during the Age of Pirates, no ship—be it Spanish, British, Danish, Dutch or French—was safe from falling prey to pirates on the high seas.

Great Britain (made up of the countries of England, Scotland and Wales) produced more than its fair share of pirates, as did France and the Netherlands. Spaniards and their ships, again, were typically the victims of piracy, but there were pirates who came from the Spanish colonies. These pirates were typically runaway black slaves who were brought to or grew up in the Spanish Caribbean and the American British colonies. Naturally, those who ran off to join a pirate crew, whether they were of European or African descent, came from the lower classes of society, and piracy was seen as a way to achieve freedom (especially if you were born a slave) and instant wealth. The first was more easily achieved—the latter was usually achieved only briefly before it was soon lost. Of course, pirates were almost all men,

Pirates battled ferociously on land and sea. *Courtesy of Adobestock.com.*

but there were also some women who joined pirate crews and distinguished themselves as able (and vicious) pirates. Most pirates died poor and from diseases they picked up through hard living or sexual contact.

As mentioned earlier, at the beginning of the Age of Pirates, piracy was a somewhat respectable profession. Initially, "pirates" were more apt to be dubbed "privateers," meaning their piracy activities enjoyed a more or less official sanctioning by a king or queen. Basically, privateers committed high-seas robbery in the service of their country, and it was seen (more or less) as an act of war. In other words, one could actually receive honors and medals for pirate—I mean privateering—activity! A perfect example of a "privateer" who actually committed acts of blatant piracy would be Sir Francis Drake of England, but we will read more about him later on.

The Caribbean was certainly the ultimate theater and haven for pirate activity. Let's face it, *Pirates of the Caribbean* didn't just materialize out of thin air. The many wooded, mountainous islands and inlets that dotted the Caribbean literally became pirate hideouts and strongholds, bases

Seventeenth-century engraving of notorious English pirate Sir Henry Morgan. He was one of the most notorious captains active during the "Golden Age of Pirates." *Courtesy of Adobestock.com.*

El Galeon Andalucia, a modern-day reconstruction of a seventeenth-century Spanish galleon. *Photograph by Carl M. Highsmith, courtesy of the Library of Congress Prints and Photographs Division.*

from which pirate ships could dart out to waylay treasure galleons. After a particularly successful period of looting treasure ships, pirates would also typically spend their riches in the rowdy and bawdy port cities of the Caribbean, as well as port cities of the southern American colonies (St. Augustine, Florida; Charleston, South Carolina; and Williamsburg, Virginia).

All of that pirate activity in the Caribbean and Atlantic means that, today, you can find pirate museums and pirate history sites all over the Caribbean, as well as in southern coastal states (in fact, Blackbeard was actually slain off the coast of North Carolina in 1718). Unfortunately, that means that, for pirate history enthusiasts who live on the West Coast of the United States, the pirate history of the West Coast is going to pale in comparison to the pirate history found in the Caribbean and on Atlantic Coast. However, that does *not* mean that there is no pirate history to be found on the West Coast of the United States.

There is certainly far more extensive pirate history connected with the Spanish ports of the Latin America Pacific Coast to the south, but that does not mean that pirate activity did not seep up to the Pacific Coast of the United States. It did. And it did so most prominently at Monterey Bay.

Ships

Ships were a major reason for the explosion of piracy between 1570 and 1730. I know what you're thinking. *Oh, come on. Do we really need to state the obvious? Do we really need an entire chapter* (albeit a short one) *that details how sailing ships played a major role in the Age of Pirates?* I think we do. And, if you think we began with an absurdly obvious statement, then get ready, because here's another one: ships loomed large during the Age of Piracy because waterways were so all-important during the Age of Pirates!

Again, you're probably thinking: *Pirates needed ships. Ships need to travel on water. Yeah, yeah, I get it—let's move on.* Well, in the words of Jerry Seinfeld, I don't think you do! Because, to simply point out that ships and water go hand in hand with the Age of Pirates is like pointing out that the Beatles were a popular pop band in the 1960s. In other words, the supposedly plain-as-the-nose-on-your-face generality doesn't begin to paint the full picture. Yes, everyone knows that ships were important to the Age of Pirates, but does everyone *truly* know how important ships were to the Age of Pirates?

Here is a simple fact: for those living in Europe, especially during the post–Christopher Columbus era, ships and boats were the life blood their nations. Still, countries like England, France and Italy were small enough that overland travel was quite easy to do—even overland travel from coast to coast, and certainly by the 1500s, Europe had been civilized long enough that several road arteries crisscrossed the continent. Once the New World came into the picture, however, good sailing ships became crucial to those nations' prosperity. Travelers needed several good sailing ships to cross the Atlantic from Europe to the New World. Why? Because countries like England, France, Spain and the Netherlands were trying to set up colonies in the New World. These ships not only had to transport colonists to the Americas, but they also had to carry building supplies and food supplies to sustain a colonial settlement. Once a colonial settlement was set up, there had to be regular ships sailing back and forth to Europe for supplies. The colonists would send payment and duties (in the form of furs, tobacco, silver and gold bullion) to their mother country, via ship, and the mother country would send resources to sustain the settlement in return. Once Spain began setting up New World settlements, this transatlantic exchange took a far more lucrative turn. Millions of dollars' worth of gold and silver bullion were being mined in the Spanish Americas and sailed across the Caribbean and Atlantic Oceans back to Spain. Does anyone see a foreshadowing of "pirates" at this point? More to come, of course, on that point.

Now that the New World was in play, there were two huge continents where overland travel was anything from hugely difficult to virtually impossible. Distances in the New World were infinitely greater than distances to travel in Europe. The New World did have some ready-made Native American trails, but there was little in the way of dirt roads

Old, decorative Asian and English dishware shards the like of which found their way to California in the holds of Manila galleons from centuries past. The shards are now in the collection of the Monterey County Historical Society. *From author's photo collection.*

Spanish galleon battles a Pacific storm. *Courtesy of Adobestock.com.*

over which wheeled coaches could travel. There were many modes of transportation; however, the best suited for traveling long distances within the largely un-blazed wilderness of the New World would have been ships. You could sail a ship and skirt the coasts, or you could travel the inland rivers and lakes via boat (a good canoe, for example). Would it surprise you to know that the ultimate treasure dreamed of by the first European explorers was *not* a city of gold but a waterway? It's true! The ultimate prize for navigators during the Age of Exploration was to discover the fabled Strait of Anian, which we will also talk about later.

It cannot be emphasized enough that during the Age of Pirates, ships were the lifeblood of civilization! Ships transported merchandise, money and supplies, as well as civilian and military travelers—often aboard the same ship. Ships also fought in major battles (would it surprise you to know that America's War of Independence was won largely because of naval strategy?). There were also fishing ships—entire fleets of European vessels would sail to the coast of Newfoundland, simply for the fishing! And there were more "unofficial" ships at sea that carried smugglers and pirates.

You're probably thinking: *Did sailing ships lose their vital importance after the Age of Pirates?* Not for a while. For some perspective: in 1818, Spanish

California was attacked by pirates, who attacked by sea. It wasn't just that the pirates attacked the Spanish capital of California by sea—it's that even as late as 1818 (long after the primary Age of Pirates had passed) there was really no other way to attack Spanish California! There were no airplanes, so there could be no attack by air. Neither could an invading army reach California by train—there were no trains in America back in 1818. There were certainly no automobiles, and an attack by horse or by foot was possible but not likely. Civilized Spanish California was *hundreds* of miles away from *any* enemy capable of transporting any kind of significant firepower (guns or cannons). For such a potential overland invader, simply reaching Spanish California would have been the enemy's "war."

For some more perspective: in 1818, there was no road (and by "road" I'm even including two-foot-wide dirt roads) that one could travel on from the eastern part of the United States out to California. In fact, there were really only two overland "roads" that one could travel on from a civilized European location to Spanish California: the almost coastal trail up from Mexico (a distance of several hundred miles) and a more recent trail up from Mexico that crossed the Rio Grande; it, too, happened to be a distance of several hundred miles, and much of that through desert. In summary, in 1818, Spanish California was cut off from the rest of the civilized world, and the best hope of reaching its capital settlement of Monterey was by sea. Even that may have taken several weeks to a few months of rough seal travel.

So, for one last time, I will state the obvious: there could not have been an Age of Pirates had this period not coincided with the Age of Ships.

1

Manilla Galleons

The Reason for Piracy in the Pacific

We have already discussed why the bulk of pirate activity took place in the waters of the Atlantic and the Caribbean, but starting in the late 1500s and stretching on into the early 1800s, some European pirates ventured farther to the west—much to their own peril—to try their luck at piracy in the Pacific Ocean. Why did they go to such lengths? Why would they put themselves and their crews in such danger? The answer can be summed up in three words: the Manila Galleons.

Historian Frank Goddio painted this scene, which took place in 1811 in Manila, Philippines:

> *In a cloud of piety and incense, the religious images of the great ship were borne in procession around the city walls. And a cacophony of bells from the parish churches, the Archbishop of Manila raised his hands to bless the Galleon…and all aboard her. Farewell ceremonies came to a climax as the harbor resounded with the firing of seven guns.…Every worthy Manileno repeated silently the phrase carefully written at the foot of each ship shipment on the galleon's manifest: "Dios Illevandolo en salvamento— God bring it to safe harbor."*

Why all this fuss from the Spanish populace of Manila? The short answer would be this: for 250 years (from 1565 to 1815) the Manila Galleons were an all-important trade, where ships carried silks, porcelain and other goods from Asia to the New World to exchange for European silver and products. The emphasis of this trade was on European silver. Was it crucial that the galleons reached their Asian (Manila) and European (Mexico) ports safely? Yes, it was important for the Asian traders, but it was far more important for the European powers (in the case of the galleons, the European power at play was, generally, the Spanish). For the Spanish government, the taxes on Chinese imports alone yielded a handsome income. As historian Eugen Lyon wrote, "The failure of even one shipment often spelled disaster, and personal fortunes rose or fell in harmony with the vagaries of the trade." In short, the Europeans who engaged in the Manila Galleon trade—primarily the Spanish, whose ships sailed the length of the Pacific Ocean, from Mexico to the Philippine Islands in Asia—stood the most to lose if a galleon failed to reach its port. Considering the journey of a Manila Galleon was a nine-thousand-mile trek across the Pacific, *each way*, there was plenty of risk that a treasure-filled galleon might meet with disaster somewhere along the perilous route. Such perils included sea storms (which could sweep up suddenly), widespread loss of the ship's crew to disease (particularly scurvy) and, of course, piracy. Because the journey was so lengthy and so filled with danger, there was typically only one galleon a year that made the round trip from Mexico to the Philippines and back. In a good year, there would perhaps be two galleons that made the trip.

The Spanish often dubbed the galleons the "China Ships" because of the insatiable desire of Spanish consumers to purchase Chinese goods. Sales in New Spain (which we know today as Mexico) produced huge profits for merchants back in Manila. Of particular popularity in New Spain was the colorful porcelain dishware and vases that were produced in China during the last years of the Ming Dynasty and into the Ching Dynasty. However, it wasn't just colorful Chinese porcelain that came back to the Spanish New World aboard the galleons. The "China Ships" also returned with skeins of raw gold-colored silk, embroidered satin bedspreads, satin cloth, copper kettles, forged ironwork, jade statues, artistic paneled screens, sandalwood chests, lacquered writing desks and figures of carved ivory.

What did the Spanish offer the Asian traders of China, Malay, Ceylon and Cambodia, who all descended on Manila to engage in trade? The answer is simple: the Asian countries, particularly China, could not get enough of Spanish silver, which was among the finest in the world. In fact, the Chinese coveted the Manila trade—and trade with other European nations—so much that they began crafting European-like wares themselves. These wares would include porcelain with European-like artwork, church

1646 illustration showing the Virgin Mary securing the safety of a Spanish galleon along the coast of Chile. This allegorical art piece highlights the prayerful fears and hopes for the safety of the trade galleons as they ventured across the Pacific. *Courtesy of the Library of Congress Rare Books Division.*

altar ware, crucifixes, Christian artwork, rosaries and even European-styled children's toys.

Yes, some of these incredibly valuable treasure ships, along with their precious cargo, were lost at sea over the 250 years of the Manila trade, but there were enough successful round trips for European nations to decide that the Manila Galleon trade was well worth the risk. Generally, the galleons enjoyed more favorable winds on their Acapulco-Manila leg. The voyage back, from Manila to Acapulco, was more treacherous because by the time the galleons had loaded up on their treasures from the Orient and got underway, their long journey would take them into the stormy fall and winter months. Because the journey back to New Spain was longer and more perilous, the galleons usually sought a safe haven on the coast of a huge North American "island," known then as "Alta California" (or "Upper California"), which was a shorter sailing distance from Asia. For many years, the galleons often made landfall at Cape Mendocino along the California coast. There, the thick timber forests along the coast were perfect for refitting ships, and the crew could rest and procure provisions

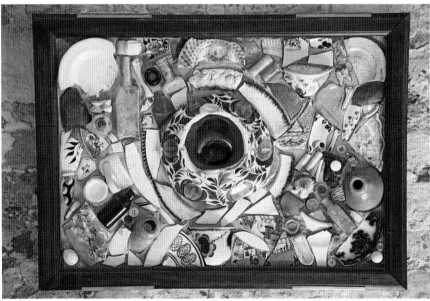

This page: Examples of Chinese hand-painted porcelain pieces, which were commonly carried in the ship holds of treasure galleons. Such pieces were coveted not only by Spanish colonists but also by English American colonists during the age of pirates. *Photographs by Carl M. Highsmith, courtesy of the Library of Congress Prints and Photographs Division.*

Early twentieth-century depiction of a ferocious pirate attack on a ship on the high seas—such as were all too common between the years 1650 and 1720. *Frederick Judd Waugh, "The Bucanneers." Courtesy of Library of Congress Prints and Photographs Division.*

(food, fresh water) for the continued journey south to New Spain. Alas, any citrus fruits, which were badly needed in order to fight the ever-present scourge of scurvy, could not be obtained until the ships reached port in Acapulco.

Why did the prosperous Manila Galleon Asia trade finally come to an end around 1815? By that time, the Spanish empire was in turmoil, and its restrictive trade policies didn't help, as other nations were getting in on the Pacific trade. Moreover, the early nineteenth century was a time when the Napoleonic Wars with Spain and the Mexican Wars of Independence (to throw off Spanish Colonial rule) were major distractions. All of these factors—not piracy—contributed to the collapse of the formerly lucrative Spanish Manila Galleon trade.

While piracy wasn't what brought the Manila Galleon trade to an end, it was a problem for Spanish authorities. Piracy was such a problem that a major step was taken in 1602 to protect the galleons from pirates, but we will learn more about that later. Just who were the pirates causing problems in the Pacific between 1565 and 1815? We will find out more about those "scoundrels" in the next chapter.

2

A Rogue's Gallery of Pacific Pirates

Considering the vast rewards that potentially awaited any enterprising pirate captain and crew who could successfully raid a Manila Galleon, it would stand to reason that the waters of the Pacific Ocean would be flooded with pirates in the years between 1565 and 1815. However, that was not the case. The reason for this is simple: to even reach the Pacific Ocean and the Manila Galleon shipping lanes, any British, French or Dutch pirate ship would have had to make a painfully lengthy and horrendously dangerous voyage from the Caribbean ports, down the east coast of New Spain and South America, around the horn tip of South America and through the perilous Straits of Magellan before finally making a trek that was hundreds of miles long up the west coast of South America and New Spain. If their ship and crew even survived the voyage, God only knew if they were in any shape to attack and capture anyone.

Despite the dangerous journey, there were some British and Dutch pirates who ventured into the Pacific in hopes of capturing a galleon, and a few of them succeeded. The most successful at this venture was the Elizabethan sea captain Sir Francis Drake.

The exploits of Sir Francis Drake, English sea captain, navigator, explorer, politician and privateer, were largely responsible for ushering in the Age of Pirates. However, in the sixteenth century, pirates (who were predominately British) were usually considered respectable "privateers"—at least by the English Crown. This meant that privateers' actions on the high seas against Spanish ships were either officially or covertly sanctioned by the English

Portrait of Sir Francis Drake, renowned Elizabethan Age explorer, privateer and possible early visitor to Pebble Beach. *Courtesy of the Library of Congress Prints and Photographs Division.*

government. In other words, the lion's share of any gold, silver or fine pearls a privateer like Drake may have "liberated" from a Spanish ship was turned over to the Crown. Still, Drake would be handsomely compensated for his efforts—probably with a cut of some of the treasure.

While Drake is known for his innumerable feats of heroism and bravery—and, yes, scoundrel-ism as well—one of his greatest accomplishments was becoming the first Englishman to sail around the world. Drake's global circumnavigation began in November 1577. Originally, Drake and his five ships had been charged to merely (and, trust me, "merely" is an understatement) sail to South America to scout out Spanish fortresses. Almost immediately after arriving off the west coast of South America, Drake had to put down a mutiny. Indeed, the Pacific leg of Drake's journey must have appeared cursed: of Drake's five ships, two were lost in storms, one turned back to England and another simply vanished! In fact, only Drake's flagship, the *Pelican*, managed to reach the Pacific. Drake would soon rename his ship the *Golden Hind*.

Drake's luck began to change, however, upon his arrival to the coast of South America above Argentina. He not only successfully attacked Spanish

Queen Elizabeth I of England, sponsor of Drake's privateering missions and world navigation voyages. *Courtesy of the Library of Congress Prints and Photographs Division.*

ports along the coast of South America, but he also captured a Peruvian treasure ship. This latter accomplishment enlightened the English to the following truth: the ultimate prize for an English mercenary vessel would be to capture a Manila Galleon.

While Drake and his crew duly attacked Spanish port towns and ships on their way up the coast of South America, Drake did not stop there. Rather than turn back to England after accomplishing his general mission, even though he had lost four ships due to stormy seas and wreckage, Drake continued up the Pacific Coast of North America in his flagship, the *Golden Hind*. One reason for Drake's decision to press on was that he was very much in search of another sort of treasure. He wanted to discover the mythical Strait of Anian, a passage across the American continent that connected the Atlantic and Pacific Oceans. To this end, Drake and his *Golden Hind* crew made their way up the coast of California in 1579.

It is well documented that Francis Drake and his men landed at a site along the northern California coast, which was probably in the vicinity of today's Point Reyes, above present-day San Francisco. Many historians believe the landing and sojourn took place, specifically, at today's "Drake's

Bay," though the exact landing site is still somewhat in dispute. It is also generally accepted that Drake and his men spent about four weeks at Drake's Bay, resting, exploring and repairing the ship. Drake claimed the territory for England and renamed the land *Nova Albion*, which means "New England." Accounts of that California sojourn also record this fact: Drake left behind a brass plate, onto which he fastened a silver sixpence coin that bore the portrait of Queen Elizabeth I. The plate announced that Drake had landed at this place and had claimed the land in the name of England and Queen Elizabeth I.

Drake and his men finally sailed from Nova Albion, never to return. They also left no trace of their stay in northern California—or so it was thought until 1933, when what appeared to be an aged brass plate with writing on it was found. The plate read:

> *BEE IT KNOWNE VNTO ALL MEN BY THESE PRESENTS*
> *IVNE 17, 1579*
> *BY THE GRACE OF GOD AND IN THE NAME OF HERR*
> *MAIESTY QVEEN ELIZABETH OF ENGLAND AND HERR*
> *SVCCESSORS FOREVER I TAKE POSSESSION OF THIS*
> *KINGDOME WHOSE KING AND PEOPLE FREELY RESIGNE*
> *THEIR RIGHT AND TITLE IN THE WHOLE LAND VNTO*
> *HERR*
> *MAIESTIES KEEPEING NOW NAMED BY ME AND TO BEE*
> *KNOWN VNTO ALL MEN AS NOVA ALBION*
> *FRANCIS DRAKE*

The brass plate and coin, which were found in Marin County, just north of San Francisco, caused much excitement among historians. Today, however, the plate has been all but proven to be a fake—in fact, it was revealed in 2003 that a man from a California history society faked the brass plate back in the 1930s as a way to prank a UC Berkeley history professor. However, for the purposes of this book, it is important that we remember this "Drake Plate," for the subject of such a discovery will turn up again later. But for now, we will move on.

There was a second Elizabethan-era English sea captain, i.e. "pirate," who was also successful in plundering a Spanish treasure ship in the Pacific. His name was Thomas Cavendish, and he, like Drake, successfully circumnavigated the globe in his vessel, the *Desire*. Cavendish accomplished this feat between 1586 and 1588. Like Drake, Cavendish also successfully attacked Spanish ships and ports as he sailed up the coast of South America. However, unlike Drake, Cavendish and his crew successfully seized a Manila Galleon, the *Santa Ana*, off the coast of California in 1587. This was almost certainly the first act of piracy to take place off the coast of today's United States!

Not all pirate attacks on Spanish ports or on Spanish galleons took place in the waters off the coast of South America or California, and not all pirates of the Pacific were of the British persuasion. In the seventeenth century, a Spanish chronicler wrote the following account about an attack—one that the Spanish did not expect would ever happen. The chronicler recorded that on December 14, 1600, a Spanish merchant vessel, the *San Diego*, "hastily outfitted for war, sailed from Manila Bay before dawn in an attempt to repel two Dutch intruders." Yes, two Dutch vessels, the *Mauritius* and the *Eendracht*, had sailed thousands of miles, across the Pacific, not for the purpose of attacking the Spanish Philippine Islands, but with the intent of capturing a Spanish Manila Galleon!

View of Point Lobos State Nature Reserve. This dramatic headland is considered by many experts to be the inspiration of Robert Louis Stevenson's pirate novel, *Treasure Island*. *From author's photo collection.*

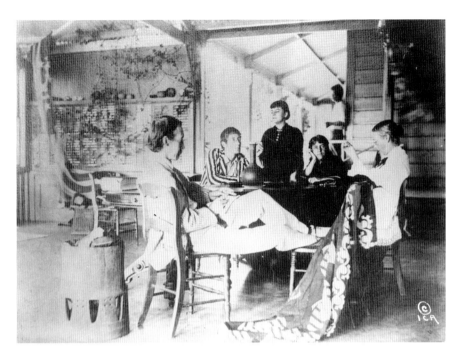

In this old photograph, Robert Louis Stevenson, author of *Treasure Island*, is seen having dinner with his family in Hawaii. This photo would have been taken around twelve years after his stay on the Monterey Peninsula. *Courtesy of the Library of Congress Online Catalogue "Stevenson, Robert Louis, 1850–1894."*

The three-hundred-ton galleon, the *San Diego*, and its companion ship, the *San Bartolome*, which bore some five hundred armed men between them, sailed out to meet the Dutch pirates, a force of about ninety armed men. In fairly short order, the *San Bartolome* defeated and took the pirates of the *Eendracht* captive. The battle between the *San Diego* and the *Mauritius* was another story, however. The Spanish crew of the *San Diego* was shocked to find that their powerful galleon was virtually powerless to fight back—the overloaded ship's cannons languished most of the battle below the water line. True, the *San Diego* also suffered for the poor leadership of Antonio de Morga, the lieutenant governor of the Philippines, who not only spent much of his time cowering behind the capstan (possibly seasick) but also ordered his leaking ship to be cut loose, after which "the sea devoured her in one fatal morsel." In the end, the *Mauritius*'s captain, Olivier van Noort, and his crew escaped for home having defeated the Spanish galleon.

After that brief (but noticeable) flurry of pirate attacks on Manila Galleons from the late sixteenth to the early seventeenth centuries, there seems to have been a lull in Pacific pirate activity. It would appear that part of the reason for this was that the Manila Galleons were better prepared to fight, dodge or outrun any would-be pirates over the next several decades. Still, as late as 1743, British commodore George Anson was so determined to capture a galleon that he and his crew sailed for three years to reach the Manila Galleon shipping lanes off the coast of the Philippine Islands. Anson's persistence paid off, as his ship, the *Centurion*, captured the *Senora de Coradonga*.

In the end, the accounts of successful British and Dutch pirate attacks on Spanish ports and Spanish galleons in the Pacific do not make for a terribly long chapter. The Pacific theater was certainly no pirate's nest—hardly a western *Pirates of the Caribbean*, but if these accounts prove one thing, it is that pirates did indeed prowl the Pacific in hopes of capturing treasure-laden Spanish galleons. That is one reason why California can indeed boast its own tales of pirate lore.

3

Treasure Island *and the Monterey Peninsula*

WHEN: 1879

WHERE: Robert Louis Stevenson House (Monterey) and Point Lobos (just south of Carmel)

Hardly anyone took any notice of the gaunt, pale-skinned young Scotsman who was once again restlessly roaming the dirt pathways of sleepy Monterey. The brunette-haired young man had been boarding at the local inn of late, an adobe house known by the locals as "The French Hotel." It was rumored that the innkeeper, Jules Simoneau, was giving the young man his meals for free, so poor was this oft-wandering vagrant. Still, the affable Scotsman purported to be a talented writer, and proved so by publishing a few pieces in the local news journal.

On this spring day of 1879, however, the Scotsman—who had of late earned the nickname "Beachcomber" for all his local wanderings—was hiking along the Monterey waterfront. He had just meandered past the long one-story adobe that, a generation earlier, had been used by local soldiers to put on plays. Now it was merely a saloon and boarding house. A few yards past this adobe, and after crossing a bridge that spanned the narrow ravine, the Beachcomber was forced to veer up onto the grassy hill which overlooked the harbor. He paused a moment to gaze back at the ancient oak tree, which now resembled a great, dying ancient octopus. A few paces in front of the tree, clinging to the ravine slope, was a weathered white cross on which was painted just one word: "SERRA." The Beachcomber had lived in this place long enough to know that this spot was revered by the local Californios; it was the place where the venerable Father Junípero Serra planted the cross upon arriving here in 1770.

A little further up the hill, the Beachcomber paused at the rubble-strewn ruins of what was once the old Spanish harbor battery. There was still a large iron cannon here, bronzed and sun-burnt, pointed out towards the water. The Beachcomber knew the old story, how the Spanish soldiers manning this battery exchanged cannon fire with Argentine pirates many years ago. The young Scotsman imagined the menacing black pirate ship in the water below, firing deadly cannon fire directly at this tiny fortress. Of course, stories of pirates were always a subject of interest to the Beachcomber. He resolved to someday himself write a truly good story about pirates.

The Beachcomber climbed further up the hill. He would visit the ruins of another fort—this one being the ruins of American Fort Mervine. It had not been located on the higher elevations of this hill for very long. Less than 40 years in fact. Yet already, the soldiers had abandoned it. There was hardly any need for a military presence at Monterey anymore. The Gold Rush had changed everything.

—Todd Cook, Nueva California

The year 1879 can hardly be considered a time one associates with pirates—smugglers, steamships and whalers perhaps. But pirates? Not so much. By 1879, that era had passed. Neither can the historical figure we will be discussing be considered a pirate by any stretch of the imagination! In fact, he was a rather sickly fellow, who was far more at home wielding a pen and inkwell than, say, a cutlass and a hook. If he did share something in common with pirates of old, it was the fact that he was not only well traveled but also (despite his tendency to frequently get sick) had a love for adventures outdoors—he liked hiking and exploring, in particular! Oh, and this little fact: popular pirate terminology, as well as the visuals many of us carry in our imaginations of the Golden Age of Pirates, come from the pen of this particular fellow. Anytime we imagine colorful buccaneers wearing dark patches over one eye, burying treasure on some wooded and rocky coastal island, and anytime we bring up phrases like "pieces of eight" or "fifteen men on a dead man's chest," we are indebted to this Scotsman who spent a few months in Monterey back in 1879. The gentleman I speak of is renowned writer Robert Louis Stevenson, who authored the world-famous pirate novel *Treasure Island* (which later became a popular Disney movie and inspired the *Pirates of the Caribbean* ride at Disneyland).

To pay homage to this celebrated Scotsman, there are two Monterey Bay locales that are essential to visit. The first is located on a narrow side street

Late 1890s photograph of the Robert Louis Stevenson House. It was named by virtue of the fact the famed author stayed at this inn for three months in 1879. *Courtesy of the Library of Congress Prints and Photographs Division, Historic American Buildings Survey.*

in Monterey. The aged structure was once known as the French Hotel, but today, it is dubbed the Robert Louis Stevenson House, after its most famous guest. Though it is hidden away, the historic two-story adobe is easily found, as it lies only one block off the major thoroughfare of upper Alvarado Street, the avenue that constitutes the heart of Monterey's downtown. One can wander the back garden and pause to gaze at the front of the former inn and boardinghouse. Better yet, there are private tours that take visitors inside the historic Stevenson House, the interior of which is filled with authentic Robert Louis Stevenson artifacts and memorabilia. While it is known that Stevenson's room was on the second floor, and while one of the rooms is redecorated to represent his actual room, it is not known for sure which upstairs room he actually resided in. Another fact should be added for the benefit of all the ghost enthusiasts out there: the Stevenson House is said to be one of the most haunted buildings in all of California.

Stevenson lodged at the French Hotel for around three months in 1879. He traveled to Monterey Bay from Scotland for one simple reason: love. The frail Scotsman was head-over-heels in love with Fannie Osborne, a woman who was still married to another man and living in San Francisco. Fannie would eventually obtain a divorce from her first husband and marry Robert Louis, but during his 1879 sojourn in Monterey, it was not certain that he would ever get to marry her. So, the lovesick young man passed his time in

Monterey writing letters to Fannie, penning literary works and enjoying free meals courtesy of nearby restaurateur Jules Simoneau, who took pity on the near-penniless Robert Louis (he had yet to make his fortune in writing). Most of all, Stevenson passed his time in Monterey by getting out on foot and exploring the Peninsula. In fact, he was seen hiking along the shoreline so much that locals gave him the nickname "Beachcomber." Stevenson hiked all through Monterey and southwest, along the shoreline, to what is today Pacific Grove (then, it was still a Methodist campground). From there, he ventured farther down the coast to explore the Del Monte Forest—today, it's more popularly known as Pebble Beach. Stevenson is said to have started a forest fire there because he was curious to see how Spanish moss would react if lit with a match. The Beachcomber also hiked over the hill to visit the ruins of the Carmel Mission before he eventually made his way out into Carmel Valley. Out in the valley, however, Stevenson suffered another bout of sickness and had to be taken in for a few weeks by a local rancher.

The Scotsman wrote about his wanderings and time on the Monterey Peninsula in his work *The Old Pacific Capital*. In this book, Stevenson also pens his account of attending mass in the ruins of the old Carmel Mission church, and he recounts the surreal discovery of the brand-new but deserted village amid the forest pines just down the coast from Monterey—this village turned out to be the Methodist campground that would eventually evolve into the town of Pacific Grove. In *The Old Pacific Capital*, Stevenson laments the rising of a huge new luxury hotel on the western edge of sleepy Monterey (the old Hotel Del Monte). What Stevenson did not write about, however, was a place that local historians strongly believe he *did* visit and was (apparently) quite taken with: Point Lobos.

You can still visit Point Lobos today—it's located off Highway 1, just south of Carmel. In fact, Point Lobos State Park and Reserve is certainly one of the most scenic coastal parks in the United States. One writer went so far as to describe Point Lobos as "the greatest meeting of land and sea in the world." It's an enchanting and—dare I say—magical place. Tall hills tower over secluded coves where blueish green waters swirl in and out among the rocks and crashing surf explodes into craggy inlets in other spots. Narrow, but hiker-friendly, trails wind along the stunning forested shoreline. There are also groves of low, but thickly rooted cypress trees, their twisted trunks half-covered with reddish-orange moss. When the trails emerge onto open rocky vista points, one can view sea gulls, barking sea lions, playful sea otters and even passing whales in the ocean below.

Views of Point Lobos State Nature Reserve. This dramatic headland is considered by many experts to be the inspiration of Robert Louis Stevenson's pirate novel, *Treasure Island*. *From author's photo collection.*

In short, Point Lobos is the perfect setting for a pirate novel, and many historians believe it did in *Treasure Island*.

Yes, the fictional island, where characters like Long John Silver, Billy Bones, Captain Flint and the lad Jim Hawkins played out the pirate saga of treasure and buccaneer mayhem, is indeed said to be based on the Monterey Peninsula's own Point Lobos. In fact, Point Lobos is said to fit the description of the fictional Treasure Island almost to the letter: the prominent island peak, the numerous secluded coves and inlets, the rocky coastline pounded by surf and the forested cliffs. In fact, the novel's description of the island far more resembles Point Lobos than it does the tropical island it is intended to be in the novel! Furthermore, the first film interpretation of *Treasure Island* (released in 1934) was actually filmed at Point Lobos!

True, Robert Louis Stevenson, as far as I know, never went on record to confirm that *Treasure Island* was inspired by Point Lobos, but most California and Stevenson historians make that connection. The novel itself was published in 1883, four years after Stevenson's time in Monterey. The author would live only another eleven years after the publication of that novel, which, perhaps more than any other work or event, inspired countless

Above and opposite: Two views of the lighthouse (historic in its own right) at Point Pinos in Pacific Grove. This headland was spotted—and noted—by, arguably, the first New World pirate in 1542. *From author's photo collection.*

generations of young people to become fascinated by the Age of Pirates—a phenomenon that still continues today.

One final note on Point Lobos pirate history before we move on: aside from the strong *Treasure Island* connection, there is no actual pirate lore connected with Point Lobos. For lovers of pirate history, that might come as a disappointment, as this enchanting coastal locale would be a perfect setting for an actual pirate tale or two. However, the history of Point Lobos is not without something *akin* to pirate activity. Beginning in the mid-1800s, long before it became a state park and nature preserve, whaler and fishermen camps dotted the shores of Point Lobos. At the same time, Point Lobos also became a focal point for more sinister activity: namely, smuggling. Yes, the many narrow, secluded, virtually hidden coves and caves found around Point Lobos were the scenes of fairly significant smuggling activity from the mid-1800s through the early 1900s, after which such shady operations were pushed out by the legitimate fish industry operations and a U.S. military installation at the site.

4

Juan Rodriguez Cabrillo

First New World Pirate

WHEN: 1542
WHERE: Point Pinos and Pacific Grove

Indeed, Alonso had been beguiled by the sight of Bahia de los Pinos since that day they had spotted it, back on the 17th of November. On this voyage they had passed other headlands where stands of pine trees grew. But Alonso had never seen pines like those that covered the headlands of Bahia des Pinos this was a headland of tall, slender pine trees with clumps of cloud-shaped greenery, inter-mixed with short, thick-trunked pines with branches that twisted into exotic shapes. To Alonso's eyes, there was something peculiarly Asian about the landscape—perhaps the topography resembled to him a scene from Asian ceramic ware and scroll illustrations. This stretch of coastline was, to Alonso's mind, more surreal and dreamlike than any landscape they had yet seen on this voyage. It had to be explored.

But that would be later. Alonso was more determined that his friend and capitán, Juan Rodriguez, be nursed back to health. Juan Rodriguez Cabrillo was too brave, too mighty a conquistador to himself be conquered by a mere broken leg. But the poison was setting in, and he was suffering badly. Alonso could not believe such a terrible thing could be happening.

On the third of January, Cabrillo was rowed ashore to the rocky, treeless island of La Posesión. It was thought best by the crew to get him off the dank and chilly ship, onto the heights of the island rocks, where the sun could shine down on his body. It did not help. In his dying words,

Rodriguez Cabrillo charged his ship pilot, Bartolomé Ferrer, to take charge and lead the expedition back north again along the coast. The search for the Strait of Anian was not to be abandoned. As Juan Rodriguez Cabrillo breathed his last, Alonso held his hand and wept bitterly.

—Todd Cook, Nueva California

Point Pinos is the farthermost point that the Monterey Peninsula extends out into the Pacific. The Point is the gateway to Monterey Bay for ships approaching from the south and is located just past the town of Pacific Grove. There, the shoreline and ocean burst forth completely into view (as opposed to being blocked by the buildings of Cannery Row in Monterey and structures of Pacific Grove). Following the coast road out to Point Pinos, one will pass quaint Victorian homes and inns, as well as Pacific Grove's famous "pink carpet" flower beds (most vivid in the spring) amid the ice plants. At Point Pinos, the landscape is marked by golf greens, sand dunes and a striking rocky shoreline, all of which comprise this historic headland.

After circling past the golf greens and sand dunes, a major landmark comes into view. Standing like a sentinel on a rise, just adjacent to the golf course, is the 1855 Point Pinos Lighthouse. This striking building is historic in its own right, as it is the oldest continuously operating lighthouse on the West Coast of the United States.

Once you've taken in the landscape and seascape of this circular Point Pinos drive or hike, you can be satisfied that you have communed not only with the ravishingly beautiful scenery but also with Monterey Bay's earliest pirate-related history, which goes all the way back to 1542. Yes, 1542—which, if you've been paying attention, *pre*-dates most accepted starting points for the Age of Pirates. But this date and the "pirate" connected with it in Point Pinos history must be included on our pirate history tour. I say this because Juan Rodriguez Cabrillo, commander of the first European expedition to explore the coast of California, might actually be the first New World pirate.

That Juan Cabrillo—who was actually Portuguese but fought and sailed in the service of Spain—could rightfully be considered a "pirate" is, I think, an unorthodox theory. At least in my research, I have never seen Cabrillo described as a pirate. A conquistador? Yes. An explorer and navigator? Absolutely. But never a pirate. Still, we should consider Cabrillo's history.

Before Cabrillo made his historic 1542 voyage up the coast of what is today the state of California (and possibly some of the Oregon coast as well), he distinguished himself in another way. Juan Cabrillo played a key role in the conquest of Mexico under the command of renowned Spanish conquistador Hernán Cortés. When the mighty Aztec capital of Tenochtitlan fell to Cortés, his soldiers and their Native allies in 1521, the first major victory in the War of the Worlds (powerful Old World civilization versus powerful New World civilization) began a chain of events whereby Mexico, Central America and South America—along with their vast riches—fell under the control and domination of the Spanish in the sixteenth century.

However, the fact is that Cortés may have failed in his quest to conquer the powerful Aztecs of Mexico were it not for the naval expertise of one of his officers: Juan Rodriguez Cabrillo. You see, despite the fact that the Spanish had made major headway in their quest to gain control of Tenochtitlan in 1519, their position in the city, where they had initially been welcomed by ruler Moctezuma and the Aztec citizenry as gods, had become precarious. The Aztecs, angered and feeling betrayed by the violent acts committed against them by the Spanish (which included taking the Aztec ruler hostage), were now openly hostile toward their Spanish "guests." The Spanish knew it was time to get out of the city.

At this point in the story, it is important to have a general visual of the Aztec city: though located in the Valley of Mexico, Tenochtitlan was completely surrounded by a huge lake. The mainland of the valley (where the lower-class Aztec population lived) was connected to the city by several bridges. It was on one of these causeways that Spanish troops were spotted by Aztec sentries as they were attempting to flee Tenochtitlan under the cover of night. Almost instantly, the Spaniards found themselves overwhelmed by Aztec warriors, who swarmed the bridge causeways on foot and from war boats on the lake. Several Spaniards were killed and taken captive, only to later be sacrificed atop the great stone temples of Tenochtitlan. Cortés lost half, if not more, of his forces—the rest (including Cortés) made it to the safety of the mainland. By all logic, Cortés and his conquest of the Aztec Empire were finished after the massacre of half his Spanish troops.

Incredibly, however, Cortés was still determined to topple the great city. Rather than try to sail back to Spanish Cuba to regroup, Cortés remained in Mexico, leading his troops up into the forested mountains. There, Cortés charged one of his officers, a skilled shipbuilder and navigator by the name of Juan Rodriguez Cabrillo, to oversee the felling of trees and the construction of attack vessels. By 1521, the herculean task was complete, and the Spaniards launched an all-out attack on Tenochtitlan—this time by water. It was a naval attack in the valley center of Mexico!

The Spanish succeeded. Their "war ships" overwhelmed the Aztec war canoes, and soon, the Spanish foot soldiers were in the city, engaging the Aztec warriors in the streets. The fighting was furious and lasted for several months, but in the end, the combination of superior Spanish firepower and (perhaps most damaging of all to the Aztecs) a deadly scourge of disease roaring through the city resulted in the weakening and, finally, slaughter of untold numbers of Aztec warriors. Mighty Tenochtitlan had fallen to the Spanish. Today, the metropolis of Mexico City stands over the ruins of the old Aztec capital. Still, Tenochtitlan was a city so spectacular in its time that many of Cortés's troops, upon seeing the city for the first time in 1519, thought they were hallucinating.

So, does Cabrillo's role in the conquest of Tenochtitlan make him a pirate? I would say that, at least in a certain sense, it does. It was Cabrillo who built the war vessels and undoubtedly had a leading role in the attack-by-water on Tenochtitlan. Granted, one could argue that this more rightly categorizes Cabrillo as a soldier instead of a pirate. But, remember, especially in the sixteenth century, the lines between a "soldier" and a "pirate" were oftentimes blurred—as are the lines between "privateer" and "pirate." Often, it was hard to tell when the fine line was crossed between privateer, mercenary and pirate. The former was done in the service of one's country—the latter could still be done in the service of one's country, but it was characterized as crossing over the line of propriety and "good form" in the pursuit of ill-gotten riches.

However, it was not just Cabrillo's leading role in an attack-by-water (and remember, Spain had never officially declared war against the Aztecs) that arguably colors him as a pirate. In any pirate attack, there is the element of plundering. In the case of the Spanish overrunning Tenochtitlan, there was definitely plundering that took place. To be fair to Cabrillo, however, it is important to note that his movements during the ground invasion of Tenochtitlan are largely unknown. Maybe he was running amok and grabbing every gold necklace or idol he could lay his hands on. Then again, maybe he spent most of his time repairing the Spanish boats used in the attack. We do know Cabrillo played a major role in the water assault on Tenochtitlan, and we know there was plundering of the city's riches following the naval assault. So, for those reasons, it's not too much of a stretch to dub Juan Rodriguez Cabrillo as *perhaps* the first pirate of the New World.

So, what does Point Pinos have to do with Juan Rodriguez Cabrillo? Well, I wish I could tell you that Juan Cabrillo and his men landed at Point Pinos, walked onto its shore and buried a chest of treasure there. But Cabrillo never set foot on Point Pinos—or anywhere on the Monterey Peninsula that we know of. What Cabrillo *did* do, however, is sail his ship within viewing distance of Point Pinos. The Point apparently impressed Cabrillo enough for him to make special note of it and to dub it *Bahia des Pinos* (Bay of Pines). In other words, unlike today (especially with the golf greens, the lighthouse and naval sub-station in place), the Point Pinos of 1542 was covered with pine trees—pines that were even described as bearing a dusting of snow.

Perhaps Cabrillo would have lingered—and even made a landing—at Point Pinos were it not for the likelihood that he was in a hurry to return safely to Mexico after his long voyage. It was the winter storm season when he passed the Monterey Peninsula, and any local can tell you that the seas around Point Pinos, especially in the winter months, can be horrendously treacherous.

Cabrillo, in fact, did not make it back to New Spain (today's Mexico and Latin America). He died from a leg injury infection while anchored off California's Channel Islands. Still, Cabrillo will go down in history as the first European to chart the coast of California—and as the first European to lay eyes on and to make a description of the Monterey Peninsula.

Before we take leave of Juan Cabrillo and Point Pinos, it should be noted that there is more to pirate history at Point Pinos than just Cabrillo's voyage. After the Spanish finally settled Monterey Bay in 1770, it was not long before a sentry post was established at the point. A soldier could spot any potential

Pebble Beach's famed Lone Cypress Tree. It is possible that two sixteenth-century "pirates" sailed right past this natural landmark even before the Pilgrims landed at Plymouth Rock. *From author's photo collection.*

An early 1900s photograph of Fanshell Beach. It was about thirty years after this picture was taken that the Drake Lead scrolls were discovered on this—or possibly nearby Moss—beach. *Courtesy of the Mayo Hayes O'Donnell Library.*

enemy ships sailing into Monterey Bay while manning the Point Pinos sentry post. Once those ships rounded the point, they had about four miles to sail before reaching the primary harbor of Monterey, the capital of Spanish and Mexican California. This would allow time for the sentry to gallop from Point Pinos to Monterey and sound off the warning.

It was from the vantage point of Point Pinos, in fact, that the enemy pirate ships of Hippolyte Bouchard were first spotted entering Monterey Bay in November 1818. More on that story to come!

5

An Elizabethan Pirate Landing in Pebble Beach?

WHEN: 1579
WHERE: Moss and Fanshell Beaches (both in Pebble Beach)

To reach our next two Monterey Peninsula pirate history sites, one must pass through the gates at the entrance to Pebble Beach. There is a fee to enter, but the visual access to stunning scenery, jaw-dropping mansions and world-class golf greens of Pebble Beach is definitely worth the price of admission. After reading this chapter, I hope you will also be drawn to the dramatic pirate history that *may* have taken place here.

   There are multiple gates through which to enter the community of Pebble Beach and drive the scenic road that is its most famous attraction: the Seventeen-Mile Drive. To reach our "pirate" sites most quickly, however, it is best to begin at the lower entrance, near the waterfront. In fact, this is the entrance one would naturally come to after visiting nearby Point Pinos. Once you have paid your admission fee and have started along the Seventeen-Mile Drive, you will first pass the Spanish Bay Resort Inn on your right, and at the first intersection past it, the Drive veers westward toward the ocean. As far as pirate history is concerned, there are two beaches you will want to visit along the Seventeen-Mile Drive: Moss Beach and the smaller, more cove-like, Fanshell Beach. Mind you, the pirate history at Fanshell Beach is the same pirate history that is connected to Moss Beach, but you will want to stop at *both* beaches since the pirate-related history that follows may have taken place at Moss Beach…*or* it may have taken place at Fanshell Beach. There are differing accounts, and as of the publication of this book, it has yet to be sorted out. That's why I say you should visit both beaches—indeed, as long as you paid your admission fee for the Seventeen-Mile Drive, there's no reason not to! As for the pirate history that takes us to Pebble Beach, it has to do with a prominent figure who was discussed earlier in this book.

For this story, we have to go back to the year of 1934. A local resident was taking a stroll along the beach when something peculiar caught his eye: a strange-looking old bottle, half-buried in the sand. Now, before we go any further, let's clarify all the beaches that we will encounter in this story. The community in which this story took place is Pebble Beach. However, the actual beach where this resident found the old-looking bottle was *Moss* Beach. However, some claim that the bottle was found on *Fanshell* Beach. Again, as to whether the bottle discovery took place at Moss Beach or Fanshell Beach—both within the *community* of Pebble Beach—accounts still differ. All cleared up? Good. Let's proceed.

After finding the bottle, the gentleman pulled it from the sand and examined it. The bottle definitely appeared to be an antique. It was heavy, filled as it was with sand. The gentleman took the bottle home, and for the

Fanshell Beach along Pebble Beach's Seventeen-Mile Drive. This is one of the potential landing spots of Francis Drake and his crew from 1579! *From author's photo collection.*

next fifteen years, it served as a bookend on his shelf. Finally, in 1949, our Pebble Beach bottle-finder discovered that the sand was beginning to seep out through a crack in the aged bottle. It was at this point that he decided to empty the bottle of the offending sand. In the process of emptying the bottle, he noticed two cylinder-like objects inside the bottle. The man lost no time in enlisting the aid of a local art store owner in removing the mysterious objects. At last, with careful use of forceps, the first object was freed from its aged container.

To the amazement of the two men, the object turned out to be a bent Elizabethan sixpence coin dating back to the late 1500s. Thrilled by the find, the local resident and art store owner were even more careful when removing the second object, a task that took about three hours. Finally, the second object in the bottle was removed. It was a peculiar-looking rolled-up piece of lead. Very carefully and deliberately, the old lead cylinder was unraveled.

Inside, there was crude writing on the lead piece. It took some time and patience to decipher, but at last, the two men were able to read the etched-in message. What they read was jaw-dropping:

IN NOMINEE ELIZABETH HIBET BRITANNA
RIAR REGINA
I DO CLAIM THIS GREAT LAND AND THE SEAS
THEREOF, THERE BEING NO INHABITANTS IN
POSSESSION TO WITNESS THERETO THIS BOTTLE
AT GREAT TREE BY SMALL RIVER AT LAT. 36 D.
30M. BEYOND HISP. FOVR OVR MOST FAIR AND
PVISSANT QVEENE AND HERRE HEIRS AND SVCCESSORS
FOREVER VNTO THEIRR KEEPING
BY GOD'S GRACE THIS FIRST DAY OF MAY 1579

FRANCIS DRAKE
GENERALI
FRANCIS FLETCHER
Scriv

If authentic, the lead scroll was nothing less than evidence that Drake had landed at Pebble Beach and claimed that part of North America for England—a full month before he had arrived at Drake's Bay in June 1579. Taking this theory a step further, if the lead scroll is to be believed, is it possible that Drake might have considered returning to the shores of Pebble Beach to establish a fort? Might Drake have even contemplated establishing a settlement there? Did Pebble Beach nearly become the site of the United States' first English settlement?

Before we get too carried away, I should tell you what the experts thought of the Pebble Beach bottle, coin and lead scroll. The bottle and its contents were sent to England to be analyzed. The findings by those experts were as follows: the bottle, which was chemically analyzed, was deemed to be at least four hundred years old, placing it squarely in the Elizabethan period. Of course, the sixpence was found to be an authentic sixpence of Elizabeth I. Despite all of this, the experts in England had their doubts as to the authenticity of the lead scroll and its message. The lead scroll was also examined by leading university experts in California. They felt the aged lead scroll was indeed authentic. So, who is to be believed, the skeptics or the believers? Even more to the point, where are the bottle, coin and lead scroll now?

Well, I'm sad to say that the "Drake Bottle" and its contents have vanished. According to the gentleman who found it, the bottle and its contents were lost when his home was burglarized in 1965. Some feel, however, that the Drake bottle, coin and scroll are not actually lost, rather, they are being kept hidden. Perhaps the finder was tired of the critics who insisted his prize was nothing more than an elaborate hoax. Perhaps the historical lead scroll will surface again someday.

We have no historical documents verifying a Drake landing anywhere on the Monterey Peninsula, much less at Pebble Beach. But his ship, the *Golden Hind*, would indeed have been in the vicinity of Pebble Beach in May 1579, therefore, an unrecorded landing cannot completely be ruled out.

In fact, the following assertion by historian Harry Kelsey in his 1998 book, *Sir France Drake: The Queen's Pirate*, is quite an eye-opener for anyone mulling over the mystery of the Pebble Beach Drake Bottle and Scroll. In his book, Kelsey points out that Elizabethan period author and promoter Richard Hakluyt once wrote, "The harbor where Drake stopped was in 38°." This claim was based on Drake's own account of the Pacific voyage, which was finally published in 1628. Specifically, that 1628 publication "locates Drake's California harbor at 38° north latitude." That means if Drake, who was using Spanish maps (as would be expected considering they last mapped the coast), actually sailed to what he thought was 38° north latitude, he may very well have sojourned not up at Point Reyes above San Francisco Bay but at Monterey Bay—which was where Cabrillo's fleet sheltered after a Pacific

Another present-day view of Fanshell Beach along Pebble Beach's Seventeen-Mile Drive. This is one of the two beaches that is said to have been where Sir Francis Drake left a bottle, coin and lead plate in 1579. *Photograph by Carol Highsmith, courtesy of the Library of Congress Prints and Photographs Division.*

Spanish Colonial History, mural by Daniel Sayre Groesbeck at the Santa Barbara County Courthouse in Santa Barbara, California. It is a fanciful painting of Sebastian Vizcaino and crew coming ashore to plant the flag of Spain on an Alta California shore in 1602. *Photograph by Carol M. Highsmith, courtesy of the Library of Congress Prints and Photographs Division.*

Pre-1905 photo of Vizcaino-Serra Oak Tree. Did English pirates literally drive Spanish explorers to this bayside landmark in 1602? *Courtesy of the Mayo Hayes O'Donnell Library.*

storm. It should be noted, however, that Kelsey also sees problems with this intriguing theory, but it something quite interesting to mull over!

The all-too-easy conclusion would be this: the famous brass "Drake Plate," which was found just above San Francisco Bay, was proved to be a fake, therefore, the Pebble Beach bottle, coin and scroll are also certainly hoaxes. Granted, creating a fake "old" brass plate with an etched message from "Francis Drake" and hiding it on the shores of northern California is one thing; it's quite another to track down a genuine four-hundred-year-old bottle, a four-hundred-year-old Elizabethan sixpence and an aged-looking lead piece in which to etch a message from *Golden Hind* ship scribe Francis Fletcher, then motor down to Pebble Beach and hide the bottle, coin and rolled-up lead plate in the sand. This would have been especially hard in the early to mid-1930s when Pebble Beach was sparsely populated and the likelihood of someone finding the bottle would have been low. This theory is plausible, I suppose, but it seems to me a huge amount of trouble and effort just for a laugh. It's also possible that the Drake landing—as well as a bit of Elizabethan pirate history—may actually have taken place on the shores of Pebble Beach. We can only speculate.

6

British Pirates and the Discovery of Monterey Bay

WHEN: December 1602
WHERE: Vizcaíno-Serra Landing Site Monument; Monterey

The last hymn had been sung. Fray Ascención said the benediction. The mass was complete. Then, the incredible moment happened. As if on divine cue, the fog lifted, revealing, for the first time, the bay in all its jaw-dropping glory: a gigantic arc of blue, surrounded on every side by wooded mountains, their slopes covered with oak and tall, slender pine trees. Innumerable ships could anchor here and be sheltered from the westerly winds by the great hills rising above the oak tree and ravine. Fresh water streams could be seen emptying into the bay at several locations, not only from the ravine behind the oak but also less than half a league away to the east. Here, truly, was the harbor he had been seeking for the last seven months!

Vizcaíno then gave the order to unfurl the colors of Spain. Moments later, the flag of España was hoisted above the lapping bay waters as shouts of, "Viva España!" filled the morning air.

"Raise the cross of Christo!" thundered Vizcaíno, and, immediately, several of the crew lifted the already-prepared wooden cross, securing it in place on the grassy hillside overlooking the bay and the oak tree. Another hymn was sung. Vizcaíno beamed with pride as the flag fluttered in the morning breeze, while, nearby, the Christian cross stood, tall and bold, overlooking the northern latitudes of Alta California for the first time. Now, it was time for Vizcaíno to complete his claim over this fabulous harbor by

giving it a name for which it would be known for all posterity. Making sure he had the full attention of his crewmen and the friars, Vizcaíno proudly made his proclamation: "By the grace of Our Most Holy Lord and Savior Jesús Christo, and in honor of the Most Esteemed and Honorable Viceroy of Don Gaspar de Zuñíga y Acevedo, Conde de Monte Rey, Don Gaspar de Zuñíga y Acevedo, Conde de Monte Rey, this most excellent harbor shall henceforth be known as the Bay of Monte Rey!"

That day, Vizcaíno offered up his own personal thanks to God for his great success. So elated was the captain at finding this wonderful harbor, that, given the chance, he would even have thanked the pirates who compelled him here.

—Todd Cook, Nueva California

Our next Monterey Bay pirate history spot is tucked away on a quiet corner of the city of Monterey, at the nexus of Pacific Street and Artillery Boulevard. Don't be afraid to enter though the tall white posts, which signify the entrance to the Army Presidio, however. You will notice there are no military sentries at this gate—that's because, when you initially enter the Presidio, you have actually entered the Lower Presidio Historic Park, which is leased to the city by the U.S. military for use as a historic park. When you pass the quiet, bucolic grass plot just outside the gate at the nexus of Pacific Street and Artillery Boulevard, note the Celtic-styled stone cross standing there. That stone cross marks the spot where Sebastián Vizcaíno and his crew came ashore and gathered under the branches of an oak tree for a Catholic mass and land-claiming ceremony in December 1602.

I should be clear: Sebastián Vizcaíno was a Spanish soldier, entrepreneur and explorer; he was *not* a pirate, and neither were the men who sailed with him (at least that I know of). Yet, the story of Sebastián Vizcaíno and his 1602 landing at Monterey Bay has *everything* to do with pirates.

In short, pirates, and specifically British pirates, were the primary reason the viceroy of New Spain commissioned Vizcaíno to sail up the coast of Alta California in search of the perfect harbor. As I discussed earlier, from the late sixteenth century to the dawn of the seventeenth century, Spain was sending yearly galleon (i.e., "treasure") ships across the Pacific to engage in a lucrative trade in Manila. These treasure ships came to be known as Manila Galleons, and each year, they would embark from ports in Mexico (usually Acapulco) and make the arduous six-month journey across the Pacific.

Today, this Celtic-style stone cross marks the approximate site where the Vizcaino-Serra Oak once stood. *From author's photo collection.*

There were no convenient stops at Polynesian islands along the way to the port of Manila—remember, the Hawaiian Islands were not be discovered by European navigators until 1778, some two hundred years after the beginning of the Manila Galleon era. Upon arrival in the Philippines, Spanish gold and silver would be traded in exchange for coveted Asian spices, cloth and decorative porcelain ware. Once the galleons were loaded with the purchased Asian goods, the ships would make the same six-month journey back to Mexico—in all, this was a full one-year process. But, starting in the late 1570s, there emerged a problem: the Spanish Manila Galleons had caught the attention of British pirates.

Throughout the sixteenth century, the Spanish had enjoyed an almost complete European monopoly in the waters of the Pacific Ocean, but that changed in 1579, when English explorer and privateer Francis Drake sailed up the Pacific coast of the New World in search of the fabled Strait of Anian (the waterway across the American continent). As long as he was "in the area," so to speak, Drake also took the opportunity to attack Spanish ships and ports in South America. Afterward, like Cabrillo before him, Drake and

his crew sailed up the coast of Alta California, stopping for a time at what many historians believe to be Point Reyes, just north of today's city of San Francisco.

After Drake's historic 1579 Pacific voyage, a new era in British piracy had begun, though it would actually prove to be a brief and fairly minor one. At that time, British privateers became aware of Spanish treasure ships not only in the Caribbean and Atlantic but in the waters of the Pacific as well. Again, British privateers and pirates were not nearly as prevalent in the Pacific as they were the Caribbean and Atlantic (the sailing distance to reach the Pacific was far greater), but they had become enough of a problem for the Spanish that, by 1602, they saw the need for a "safe harbor" for their Manila Galleons on the northern coast of the still-mysterious and unsettled Alta California coast.

The basic idea of the harbor was this: the Manila Galleons would set sail from the Mexican port of Acapulco (part of New Spain at the time) in February or March of each year, make the six-month voyage to Manila to do trade, then sail back along a shorter route to a Spanish harbor on the coast of Alta California. There, the crews could rest, the ships could be re-fitted and, finally, Spanish man o' war ships could escort the galleon through (presumably) pirate-infested waters, safely back to port in New

Spain. In other words, what was planned for the Alta California safe harbor, as Vizcaíno would come to find, was for it to be the establishment of a Spanish port city. Ideally, this port city would be a naturally protected harbor, a strong fort with a Catholic mission and pueblo (town) adjacent to the fort. Well, in December 1602, Vizcaíno found his perfect Alta California safe harbor, the one he named the Bay of Monte Rey—so named after Gaspar de Zúñiga Acevedo, viceroy of New Spain, who was otherwise known as the Count of Monterrey.

Upon his return to New Spain in 1603, Vizcaíno made a glowing report of his Bay of Monte Rey discovery to the viceroy. He described a beautiful natural harbor "sheltered from all winds" that was so large it could easily accommodate several fleets of ships. The well-watered mountains, which surrounded the harbor on all sides, were thickly forested with tall trees, perfect for refitting ships. And the natives they encountered were docile and friendly. The viceroy liked what he heard, and he gave Vizcaíno permission to move forward with the planning of the Bay of Monte Rey fort and settlement.

Soon after, however, the plans for the new Alta California port, pueblo and presidio came to a sudden halt when the Count of Monterrey died in 1605. The new viceroy's ideas for Vizcaíno and Alta California were completely different from those of his predecessor. The new viceroy, as it turned out, had little confidence in Vizcaíno. For one, he was not pleased that Vizcaíno had taken it upon himself to rename all the natural landmarks along the coast of California that Cabrillo had named in 1542. Secondly, the new viceroy suspected that Vizcaíno was exaggerating his claims and accomplishments in order to bolster his standing. Lastly, the new viceroy simply believed that establishing a port way up at the Bay of Monte Rey—a seven-month journey—was simply not worth the effort and expense. Plans for an Alta California port were indefinitely tabled. In fact, Alta California (what we know today as the state of California) was left unsettled by Europeans for the next 168 years.

Nevertheless, the Bay of Monte Rey—which eventually became known as Monterey Bay—had been discovered, and it lived in legend in the collective minds of the Spanish from 1602 to 1770. For more than a century and a half, mariners could only wonder aloud about this magnificent, Shangri-La-like natural harbor that Vizcaíno and his crew had discovered. The Bay of Monte Rey would finally be rediscovered in 1770—and while it still proved to be a beautiful bay and exceptional harbor, it turned out that Vizcaíno had indeed exaggerated his reports.

The bay is not completely surrounded by wooded mountains on all sides and sheltered from all winds. There are not—nor were there ever—gushing freshwater rivers cascading down high mountain ravines into the bay (there are creeks cascading down from some low surrounding hills). In the end, the Spanish finally did settle the Bay of Monterey, and it became the capital, as well as the religious and cultural center, of California from 1770 until the Gold Rush years of the 1850s. Perhaps we should thank the British pirates for driving Vizcaíno there in the first place.

In closing, one can only ponder what the history of Monterey Bay would have been had the Count of Monterrey not died in 1605. What if the Spanish—led by Vizcaíno—had indeed established a Manila Galleon port in the early years of the 1600s at the Bay of Monte Rey? It is safe to say that Monterey Bay would have had a much longer and, almost certainly, more colorful history. A galleon port, as was planned, would almost certainly have attracted the British pirates that plagued Spanish shipping efforts. Is it a stretch of the imagination to picture this hypothetical seventeenth-century fort and pueblo at the Bay of Monterey being bombarded by pirate cannons? Had this port settlement indeed materialized in the early years of the 1600s, one can only wonder if Monterey Bay's colonial history would have more resembled the raucous Disney ride depiction of a Caribbean port town being ransacked by pirates (only not nearly so cute as Disney portrays). In other words, in an alternate universe, the port of Monterey might have become a magnet—perhaps even a haven—for pirates. The settlers and natives of Monterey Bay would undoubtedly have suffered in such an environment and perhaps would have lived in constant fear.

The Oak

Remember our Celtic-styled stone marker on the grass plot at the corner of Pacific Street and Artillery Boulevard in Monterey? That's the spot where one needs to stand and ponder pirate-related Vizcaíno history, because that is where "The Oak" once stood, more or less. I say that because, if you stand in front of that stone cross today, you have to imagine the ground dropping out from under you, revealing a fifteen-foot drop to the bottom of a ravine below—the waters of the bay actually would have been washing up into the entrance of the ravine below in 1602. Below the cross—about six or seven feet below today's ground level—is where the base of the oak tree would have been, clinging to the grassy slope adjacent to the ravine. To put it another way, the site, as it appears now, is quite different than how it appeared in 1602. Back then, where the stone cross now stands there would have been a steep hillside dropping down to the bay waters. Today, the stone cross stands on a level grass plot, several yards away from the waterfront. This is because of significant landfill for railroad tracks and concrete roadways that started in the late 1800s. The ravine itself still exists—you can see it just a few paces behind the stone cross—but the ravine has filled in quite a bit since the 1600s and 1700s. It no longer empties into the bay (or it does—just a trickle's worth—because it now has to pass through a long culvert).

As for "The Oak," it was otherwise known as the Vizcaíno-Serra Oak because both Vizcaíno and Father Serra held mass beneath the branches of that oak in 1602 and 1770, respectively, and it stood where the stone monument now stands. Don't look for any image or inscription about Vizcaíno on the stone monument—there is none. The monument, erected in the early 1900s, does depict, however, a Celtic-styled cross, an image of Father Serra and a rendering of the Carmel Mission. You're probably thinking: *But what happened to the historic oak tree?* Well, it continued to stand over Monterey Bay until 1905, when it died. That year, utility workmen accidentally chopped down the venerated oak and tossed it in the bay. Fortunately, the main trunk was found bobbing in the bay and was fished out at the insistence of an aghast local priest. Today, trunk remnants of the historic tree can still be viewed at the Royal Presidio Chapel Heritage Center in Monterey and also at the Carmel Mission. A crude chair fashioned from remnants of the oak is also on display at the Pacific Grove Museum of Natural History.

I think the following bit of little-known Oak-related history is well worth mentioning. Bear in mind that the actual Vizcaíno landing date at Monterey Bay was December 17, 1602. Vizcaíno and his crew lingered at Monterey Bay to rest and explore for another two weeks—in fact, they were the first Europeans to view the Carmel Valley. They did not sail away until January 3, 1603. In other words, in all likelihood (I say "likelihood" because there is no written account of such an observance) the first Christmas celebration in California took place at Monterey Bay, very likely at the Oak site. Who knows, the Vizcaíno-Serra Oak may very well have served as California's first Christmas Tree!

Before we move on from our story of the Vizcaíno-Serra Oak Tree and the pirate history that surrounds that historic landing, I should mention one final thing. For this information, we have to go back again to the epic Spanish conquest of Tenochtitlan. Words can hardly describe the immensity and world-changing significance of that clash between the mighty powers of Spain and the Aztecs. It staggers the imagination just to picture in one's mind the awesome cityscape of the Aztec capital city, the sky red with the fires of burning temples, the clash of Spanish conquistadors and Aztec warriors as they battled amid wide avenues lined with brightly colored murals and bodies dropping into the once picturesque canals of the city. The images seem too surreal, too incredible—even too horrible—to believe that they actually took place. But it all did indeed happen, and it led to further Old World versus New World clashes between the Spanish and the Mayans, the Inca and the pueblo Indians of the Southwest United States.

What does all of this have to do with our quiet little shaded corner of Monterey where the stone monument now stands and where Vizcaíno once came ashore and claimed the harbor for Spain? Well, the Battle of Tenochtitlan actually has little to do with the Vizcaíno landing at Monterey Bay in 1602. However, if you stand at the stone monument site, think upon this: you are actually standing where the Spanish conquest of the New World—which truly began in earnest at the epic conquest of Tenochtitlan—finally came to an end. Note that I said the Spanish conquest

A rather fanciful depiction of the Vizcaino-Serra Oak, serving as the ceremonial spot for another historic mass; this one was at the founding of Monterey in 1770. *Courtesy of the Mayo Hayes O'Donnell Library.*

of the New World—which includes vast swaths of the entire mainland of North, Central and South America, as well as the Caribbean islands—not just California. That's saying quite a lot! No, this did not happen in 1602 with Vizcaíno, but it did in 1770 with the arrival of Gaspar de Portola and Father Serra at Monterey Bay.

Remember, the stone marker site is not just where Vizcaíno came ashore, celebrated mass and claimed the harbor for Spain in 1602; it is also where Gaspar de Portola and Father Junipero Serra, leaders of the 1769 expedition to *finally* settle Alta California, came ashore, said mass and claimed the land and harbor for Spain. Unlike Vizcaíno and his crew, Father Serra and the soldiers who accompanied him stayed. True, they had already planted the flag and established a presidio and mission at the Bay of San Diego (California's first settlement), but the Bay of Monterey was *always* their ultimate objective. From there, Alta California would be governed, and it is there that Father Serra would establish his mission headquarters. To summarize: the Spaniards did not consider Alta California to truly be under their control until the Bay of Monterey was settled. Yes, the Spanish would extend their settlements—

Two views (*above and opposite page*) of Carmel River Beach from two sides of the Carmel River. On this beach, amazing artifacts have been found that hint at possible pirate-era shipwrecks! *From author's photo collection.*

mainly in the form of new missions—even farther north into California after the founding of Monterey (San Jose, San Francisco, San Rafael), but I assert that these were more a case of filling-in-the-blanks of a territory already in hand than new conquests. Furthermore, never again (after the founding of the settlement at Monterey) would the Spanish claim, conquer and permanently settle a significant swath of territory in the New World.

That being the case, and granted, not every California historian will make this assertion, what began at Tenochtitlan actually *ended* at Monterey at the site of the stone monument at the corner of Pacific Street.

For a final bit of irony, let's bring our—arguably—first New World "pirate," Juan Rodriguez Cabrillo, back into the discussion. As we learned earlier, Cabrillo was the first European explorer to lay eyes upon and make note of the Monterey Peninsula, even if he didn't sail in as close to Monterey harbor as Vizcaíno later did. It is interesting to ponder the fact that Cabrillo, who played a major role in the toppling of the Aztec Empire—thus beginning, in earnest, the Spanish conquest of the New World mainland—unknowingly also laid eyes upon and noted on his map for prosperity the very forested and deserted coastal shore where the Spanish conquest of the Americas would quietly come to an end some 240 years later.

7

A Carmel Bay Pirate Shipwreck?

WHEN: Exact Date Unknown (circa 1700–1760)
WHERE: Carmel River Beach

There were three types of ships that played a role in pirate history: actual pirate-manned "pirate" ships, trade ships that were preyed on by pirates and military ships that hunted down pirates. To complicate matters further, the second and third types of ship could be turned into full-fledged pirate ships if they had the misfortune to be overrun and captured by pirates. One of these three types of ships may have met its end in the vicinity of today's Carmel River Beach.

Carmel River Beach is a picturesque stretch of white sand nestled next to where the Carmel River (which actually extends several miles into Carmel Valley) empties into Carmel Bay. That is, except at those times of year where sand bars block the river's access to the ocean. If you stand on the sands of the beach, just next to the river waters, you can look across and see a brush-covered hillside on the opposite side of the river. At the top of the nearest hill, you can see a prominent wooden cross. This cross is a re-creation of the wooden cross erected on that same hillside in 1769 by the nearly starved land expedition of Gaspar de Portola as they searched for the fabled Bay of Monterey. Not only did Portola plant a large cross at this spot, but he and his men also camped there for a couple of weeks in December 1769, hoping in vain that a Spanish supply ship would finally meet them there as planned. Unfortunately, that ship was lost at sea. Still, the cross was meant to signal to the supply ship that Europeans were in distress and encamped on that shore. So, the cross was hardly a pronouncement of conquering Christianity (as so many erroneously assume today) so much as it was a plea for help.

While that 1769 land expedition is an incredible story in itself (because it resulted in the European discovery of San Francisco Bay), it is not the pirate history story with which I am concerned. The (possibly) pirate-related history that took place on this beach may have taken place as much as a century before Portola and his men camped there. Why do I say this? Well, there is evidence—granted, the evidence is scant—that there was an old shipwreck off the shores of this beach. Was it a pirate ship? Was it a ship being chased by pirates? Was it simply a galleon trying to reach its home port in New Spain before disaster struck?

First, there is the shipwreck evidence of the old vessel itself. Apparently, the wreck predates 1769, possibly by many decades and perhaps even a century or two. Historians know this because the metallic remains of an old shipwreck were discovered by the Portola expedition of 1769. Father Juan Crespi, one of the early missionaries who accompanied Father Serra to establish the first missions in California, reported the finding in his diary:

> *Saturday, December 9—The storm lasted all day until night, when it cleared up. The California Indians who are with the expedition found on the beach an iron hoop, very large and much worn, which, when it was new, must have weighed several arrobas. It is thought it must have come from some ship's mast.*

It must be remembered that when this aged iron ship's mast hoop was discovered on the shores of Carmel Bay in 1769, no European was officially known to have set foot on the shores of Alta California since the year of 1602. However, it was generally known that in that quiet 1602–1769 timespan, Manila Galleons sometimes sailed south along the coast of Alta California from, approximately, Cape Mendocino on the coast of northern California to the Spanish port in Acapulco, Mexico. In other words, the found remains of that wreck could easily date to the raucous Age of Pirates (1570 to 1730).

Then there is a second piece to the Carmel Bay "pirate" shipwreck puzzle: a "pirate coin" discovered near that very same shore. Unlike the metal hoop piece found in 1769, the coin was discovered only a little more than a decade ago by a local gentleman named Garland Vanderpluym. As to the exact spot where Garland made this amazing find, I do not know; good treasure hunters are not prone to giving away their secrets, but Garland did confirm that the spot was at or near where the Carmel River empties into Carmel Bay. Why do I call the piece in question a "pirate" coin? Because it is a type of silver coin usually associated with pirates, pirate lore and pirate treasure. The coin I speak of is the silver Spanish "cob."

Just what is a Spanish "cob?" A cob is a crudely struck Spanish silver coin from the Spanish colonial mints of the New World. The reason cobs were so crudely struck is that the Spanish were mining *enormous* amounts of silver from their mines in Mexico, Bolivia and Peru (among other places in Latin America) during the colonial period, which then had to be sliced up into strictly weighted, but not necessarily carefully crafted, silver coins. The coin-makers (often Native American slaves) would slice chunks of silver off of a large silver bar and hammer that chunk into something resembling a round coin, but they more often resembled a triangular or rectangular-shaped coin, and they would then stamp designs on the front and back of the coin. Specifically, the "cabo" was the clump of silver sliced off the end of a silver bar, hence the English term "cob."

These ultra-crude "cob" silver coins were struck in denominations of half-reale, one-reale, two-reales, four reales and eight reales. The large eight-reales cob coins, despite their crudity, were coveted world trade and bullion coins, and they were accepted in ports around the globe. Sometimes, cob coins would stay behind in the New World to circulate as money, but for the most part, they were gathered up, packed into sturdy wooden chests and shipped back to Spain, where they would be melted and often re-coined for a hefty profit. They were also loaded onto Manila Galleons to be used in the Asia trade.

A Jerusalem cross adorns one side of all Spanish cob coins, while the other side might show rulers' monograms, a shield of arms or the Pillars of Hercules, depending on the New Spain mint. As for the size of the silver cob coins, the half-reale coin was slightly larger than today's U.S. dime, while the eight-reales was sometimes larger in diameter than even the hefty U.S. silver dollars that circulated in the days of the Old West. In fact, if you've ever heard the term "pieces of eight" (if you have ever read Robert Louis Stevenson's pirate novel, *Treasure Island*, or seen a movie adaption, then you are no doubt familiar with the term), that actually refers to the eight-reales Spanish silver cob coin. During the Age of Pirates, scoundrels of the sea constantly hoped to capture a treasure chest filled with not only gold doubloons but also silver "pieces of eight." At that time, those "pieces of eight," as well as their smaller denomination siblings, would have been Spanish cobs.

 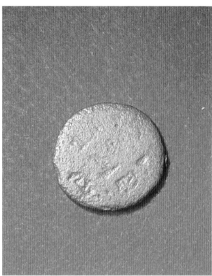

Left: The U.S. penny next to the Spanish cob. This image shows the approximate size of the artifact. *From author's photo collection.*

Right: The much more worn (reverse side) of the same Spanish cob. *From author's photo collection.*

This all brings us back to the Spanish silver cob coin found near the mouth of the Carmel River by Mr. Vanderpluym. I happen to know a thing or two about this coin because, for a couple of weeks back in 2006, I was fortunate enough to be the caretaker of this coin. At the time, I was publishing my first book, *Uncovered: The Lost Coins of Early America*, and because of that, Mr. Vanderpluym, through a good friend of mine who is a Carmel Mission docent, allowed me to take possession of the coin for a short time so that I could examine it up close. The coin did indeed appear to be a hammered coin, but the quality of the roundness was superior to that of most Spanish silver cob coins. In other words, this coin actually had the appearance, if not the perfection, of being round-shaped. The coin was a bit larger than a modern U.S. quarter in diameter, but it was a good deal thicker. This would seem to indicate that the cob was of the two-reales denomination, though, with cobs, one sometimes has to guess at the denomination from the rough diameter size. The Jerusalem Cross obverse design, along with some ornamentation near the edges, was bold and easily discerned. The reverse was quite worn and rough-surfaced, but there appeared to be some remnant of a pillar design. That would point to this cob being a product of either the mint of Potosi, Bolivia, or Lima, Peru.

A couple of things about the coin, however, did give me pause. For one, there was the overall brownish color of the coin. Oftentimes, a silver coin that tones overall brown turns out to be a copper or low-grade silver contemporary counterfeit (meaning a counterfeit struck in roughly the same period as the genuine article and meant to circulate as the genuine article), because an official Spanish two-reales cob would never have been made of either of these materials. Also, it must be noted that to numismatists and advanced coin collectors, an eighteenth-century contemporary counterfeit is usually considered to be as much a circulating coin of the period as the official coin it imitates! Why? Because back in the early to mid-1700s, coins were the primary medium of circulation in most advanced civilizations (there were no credit cards and paper money was not yet plentiful). As it happens, chances are high that as much as one-third of the coins in Europe and the Americas were counterfeit.

However, if this cob coin found near the Carmel River is actually a modern counterfeit (made to fool collectors, not to circulate as a coin of the period) then that's a different story—not to mention, highly disappointing. In that case, the coin would more aptly be called a "replica," though replicas are a technically also counterfeits. The fact is, a "replica" has little to no collector value, minimal numismatic study value and no historical value. For the most part, replicas are simply souvenirs. Granted, I did wonder if this coin might actually be a modern replica (cobs have most certainly been copied in modern times as souvenir pieces)—maybe even an aged modern replica from the early to mid-1900s. However, I simply don't believe that to be the case. The coin has too much the look of authentic age to it, and besides, I have never seen a modern replica that showed such heavy wear as is seen on the nearly obliterated reverse (modern replica designs are ultra-boldly struck and tend not to thoroughly wear off, even over seven or eight decades).

So, let's say this piece is a genuine Spanish silver two-reales cob, one struck at Potosi, Bolivia, or Lima, Peru. When was the coin was struck? Can we narrow it down to a date or date range? Well, first of all, no date was visible, even though sometimes one can make out the date on a cob coin (but often that is a tall order, even on non-worn pieces). There is, however, a hint as to the approximate date: the Jerusalem cross on the coin obverse. The Jerusalem cross appears on most Spanish silver cobs that were struck between the mid-1500s and the late 1700s. However, the Jerusalem cross on the Spanish silver cobs of the 1700s are noticeably thicker than those on 1500s and 1600s Spanish silver cobs. The cross on this Carmel River cob coin is thick, thus, I would roughly date the piece to the 1700 to 1760 date range (I stop at 1760 to give the found iron hoop time to "age" at least a little bit, before the Portola expedition found it in 1769). So, given the obverse and reverse design, the style and thickness of the cross and the more nicely round shape of this cob piece, I believe we can make the following educated guess: the coin is a silver two-reales cob of Potosi, Bolivia, or Lima, Peru, and it was struck roughly between 1700 and 1760.

Some coin enthusiasts out there might be confused by the late date of 1760 for a cob—after all, New Spain mints were striking milled, non-cob, pillar-design silver coins starting in 1732. This is true, and after the 1730s, the Mexico City mint had stopped striking cobs altogether, but that was not the case for the New Spain mints of Bolivia and Peru—from the 1730s or 1740s through 1770, both mints struck milled silver coins as well as cob silver coins.

What if the cob coin found at the Carmel River is a contemporary counterfeit? Well, that opens a whole host of new (and headache-inducing) possibilities. For one, I wouldn't be able to say whether the coin was made in Bolivia or Peru; a counterfeit could have been struck by a blacksmith at Mexico City, in the jungles of Colombia or even at the nearby Carmel Mission. It also means, as an illicit counterfeit of a coin that was still accepted in circulation, that it could have been struck anywhere from the early 1700s to even the mid-1800s. Now I'll throw another wrench into the works, particularly with the "contemporary counterfeit" scenario. For the most part, and if the coin is a contemporary counterfeit, I can only assume the piece is an imitation of a silver cob coin. That's mainly because an expert detected silver in the makeup of this coin. Were it not for the silver detected in the composition of this artifact, however, I might assume this coin is a contemporary counterfeit of a Spanish-colonial gold coin of the 1700 to 1760 period. Yes, in all of the discussion surrounding Spanish *silver* cob coins, I have neglected to discuss the Spanish-Colonial *gold* coins that were also being struck in the mints of Bolivia and Peru. The fact is, however, that this Carmel River cob more resembles a gold coin of Bolivia and Peru—same basic design as the silver cob coins, but the gold coins tended to be more nicely round. The Carmel River Spanish cob coin is indeed thicker and more nicely round than would be the typical *silver* cob coin of the period. In short, if this piece *is* an early 1700s to mid-1800s contemporary counterfeit,

Left: Obverse (front side) of a Spanish cob found in the vicinity of Carmel River Beach in 2006. Silver Spanish cob coins were standard "pirate treasure" coins. *From author's photo collection.*

Below: An 1820s view of post–Bouchard attack Monterey. Where, in 1818, there was only a fort, in this image, there is now a proper town. *Courtesy of the Mayo Hayes O'Donnell Library.*

The grassy mound at the far end of the hillside is where El Castillo, a Spanish-period harbor battery, once stood. The only land-to-sea battle in the history of California took place here when the soldiers manning El Castillo battled revolutionary invaders in 1818. *From author's photo collection.*

it might just as easily have been meant to imitate a *gold* Spanish coin as opposed to a silver Spanish coin, even if there is some silver in the piece.

Clearly, there is more studying that can be done on this mystery coin. Others have examined it, and one expert coin dealer absolutely believed a solid silver cob could turn brown after being immersed in sand, mud and water for centuries. Another expert in Spanish coins leaned toward the coin being a contemporary counterfeit (though he did not specify as to whether a counterfeit of a gold or silver cob), and as I have stated before, one expert tested the metal of the coin and found it to contain silver. So, what does this all add up to? A piece of metal ship wreckage and a Spanish cob were found in 1769 in the vicinity of Carmel River Beach and the Carmel River. Granted, that does not necessarily mean the coin and the metal shipwreck pieces are related—but that they might be connected is a tantalizing possibility. Perhaps the Spanish cob coin is from the same shipwreck as the metal piece, and perhaps that wreck was that of a pirate ship or a ship fleeing from (or hiding from) pirates. Could the wreckage and coin possibly even predate 1700? The shipwreck very possibly could have predated 1700, but it is not likely that the coin did.

There are all kinds of scenarios for the wreckage and coin: they may be connected to each other but not have any relation to pirates or fleeing ships, they may have come from different time periods within the Age of Pirates or they may be disconnected altogether. Who knows, the coin may have even been carried and lost at the spot by a soldier of the 1769 Portola expedition to settle California.

We may never know for sure, but the great thing about history and historical research is that, oftentimes, the truth eventually surfaces—whether it happens intentionally or by accident. In the meantime, it doesn't hurt anything to let your imagination run wild.

8
Bouchard Attack on Monterey, Part 1

WHEN: November 1818
WHERE: Site of El Castillo and Monterey Lower Presidio Historic Park

Having said his tearful goodbyes, Diego joined his son-in-law, Mariano Constanso, his father, old Manual Constanso (now rudely pulled out of retirement) and twenty-five other calvarymen. Led by Ensign Joe Mariano Estrada, this minute fighting force rode the one-mile distance down the beach, then up the grassy and rocky knoll overlooking the harbor. Here, they would take their posts, manning the diminutive open-sided and yellow-bricked fortress of El Castillo. Here, the Spanish force of less than thirty men, armed with swords, muskets and twelve cannons pointed out over the water, awaited the pirate fleet.

Hours later, in the darkest hour of morning, it appeared: an ominous black warship gliding slowly into the harbor. The ship came to a stop just below El Castillo. For what seemed like an eternity, it was eerily still.

"What flag is that?" a young soldier asked Diego.

Diego shook his head, "I cannot tell. It does not look familiar to me."

"It is an insurgent flag," spoke up Sargent Vallejo. At that moment, the sound of someone calling up to the fort from the bow of the black ship could be heard.

"What is he saying?" asked Diego.

"He orders us to surrender," replied the soldier next to him.

Now Comandante Estudillo took charge. "No one answer the ship! We shall address the ship at dawn in accordance to our official policy of port. But if they fire on us tonight, we shall return fire."

This was not good. Diego knew El Castillo could in no way withstand a concentrated attack. And he knew there had to be more than just this one ship. Diego crossed himself, now certain that on this night, he would surely meet his death.

—*Todd Cook, Nueva California*

If you elect to visit multiple Montery Bay pirate history sites on one excursion, a visit to the old El Castillo site would be your logical next stop after visiting the Vizcaíno-Serra Landing and Oak Tree site, because it is located just up the hill from them. In fact, after visiting the Vizcaino-Serra Oak Tree, the El Castillo site can be reached by foot—simply head through the white posts and make your way up the hill until the road veers into the Lower Presidio Historic Park. In this area, there is a grassy expanse that overlooks Monterey Harbor. The most prominent landmark visible is a stone statue of Father Junipero Serra standing with a cross in a boat (about to step on shore at Monterey for the first time).

Just beyond the granite statue of Serra, at the far edge of the grassy overlook, the terrain noticeably rises into a kind of U-shaped, grassy mound. At the edge of the mound, on the side overlooking the bay, there is a cement block marking the spot where a Spanish cannon was once fastened to its post. This is the site of El Castillo, a small fort that was manned in this spot from 1792 to 1846. El Castillo basically guarded the entrance to Monterey Harbor from the Spanish to Mexican period of California history. After that, the Americans took over Monterey, and they built their fort (Fort Mervine) farther up the hill behind El Castillo.

In its heyday, El Castillo was not the grassy mound you see today. Originally, it was described as a crude log fort, but by the first decade of the 1800s, it had developed into a fortress of mustard-yellow brick ramparts. By the Mexican period, there were even sentry and ammunition structures within the fort. All of that is gone today, but the remains of the brick footings are still underneath the grass at the El Castillo site.

The truth is, from 1792 to 1818, the Spanish sentries who manned El Castillo must have been bored silly, because there was virtually *no* action at the tiny fort during all those years, aside from a friendly visit courtesy of a British exploration expedition in 1792. It is important to remember that

Another view of the grassy knoll (just yards away from the El Castillo site) overlooking Monterey harbor and today's Fishermen's Wharf. *From author's photo collection.*

These cannons mark the site of the American fort, Mervine, which was located up the hill from Spanish El Castillo. *From author's photo collection.*

Just paces away from the El Castillo site, this cross marks the approximate spot where Alexius Nino, a black Spaniard, was buried in 1770. He was the first non-indigenous person to be buried above San Diego. *From author's photo collection.*

despite the fact that Monterey was the Spanish capital of Alta California, it was still very much located at the far edge of the civilized world. To call Spanish-period Monterey "remote" would be an understatement. To be stationed at Monterey would be something akin to being stationed at the North Pole today—only without the sub-zero temperatures.

As for the "City" of Monterey itself during the Spanish period, it was no city at all; it wouldn't even be considered a town by today's standards. There were no streets or avenues, no merchant shops, no restaurants, not even an inn (only the Carmel Mission over the hill served as a true "inn" at Monterey Bay during the Spanish-Mexican era). The City of Monterey, during the Spanish period, was the main fort, otherwise known as the Presidio, which was separate from El Castillo—El Castillo was merely a sentry fort overlooking the harbor. The Presidio of Monterey was located a little over a mile away from El Castillo and was not located where the present army Presidio is today (a point of some confusion for many present-day visitors). Residing in the Presidio of Monterey was the governor of Alta California, as well as the family of the governor. The soldiers and their families, as well as some Native American servants, also lived and worked within the walls of the Presidio. In short, the Presidio of Monterey *was* the city of Monterey during the Spanish period. Spanish Monterey was basically a wilderness frontier outpost, located in a spot that was a six-month sailing journey away from the nearest major post of civilization, Mexico. To isolate Spanish Monterey even further from the civilized world, New Spain authorities generally did not allow its citizens to trade with foreign countries.

What did all this mean for the soldiers charged with manning El Castillo from 1792 to 1818? It meant that they sat up, drilled and gazed out at a virtually empty bay for days, months and even years at a time. Only rarely would they ever see a ship entering the harbor—even then, it was usually the annual Spanish supply ship that bore much-needed resources for the Presidio and Mission San Carlos (located five miles over the hill from the Monterey Presidio). When a ship did enter the harbor, the soldiers at El Castillo would at least get the opportunity to fire off a cannon salute.

All of that changed in November 1818.

By the dawn of the 1810s, the Spanish Empire was in crisis. Its coffers were becoming depleted from its involvement in wars and its overextension of Spanish colonialism into the far reaches of the world. To cause even more turmoil, from 1808 to 1813, not only was Spain partially occupied by the French, but a Frenchman (Napoleon Bonaparte's brother, Joseph) also sat on the Spanish throne. In the 1810s, revolution was in the air, not only in Spain (against the French ruler forced upon them) but in Spanish Latin America as well. In the case of the latter, sentiment had exploded in favor of throwing off Spanish rule by a people who were demanding independence.

As for what all of this meant for Spanish California, the primary consequence was that, starting in 1810, the yearly supply ship was no longer sent from Mexico (still the capital of New Spain) to Alta California. This was a true sign that, at least in the eyes of the Spanish authorities, Alta California was on its own. Luckily, by this point, the California missions had grown and prospered enough that they not only had more than enough to support themselves, but they also had enough to provide the five California presidios with food and daily essentials. One problem remained however: there was an unprecedented threat of attack.

From 1769 to 1818, there had never been any real threat against Spanish California. The other maritime powers of the world were simply too far away to consider launching an attack on Alta California, which was basically a wilderness collection of missions and a few crude presidios spread out over several hundred miles. However, all of this had changed by the 1810s. There were now armed anti-Spanish revolutionary forces just to the south of Alta California, and it was only a matter of time before they turned their attention toward Spanish California. During this period, the people of Monterey were generally divided into two camps: those who believed an attack on Monterey was imminent—after all, it *was* the Spanish capital of the Alta California territory—and those who believed Monterey was still too small and too distant to be considered worth the time and effort of an attack. It was those in the first camp who were to be proven correct.

It wasn't that Hippolyte Bouchard, leader of the Argentine revolutionary force that sailed up to attack Monterey, was determined to launch a full-out attack on the California capital. Initially, he didn't think an attack would be necessary. And why should it have been? If the governor had been smart, he would have immediately surrendered the capital city of Alta California, retreated back to New Spain and, from there, returned in exile to Old Spain. As for the soldiers and civilians, if they had been wise, they would simply have joined the revolution! Well, if that's what Bouchard was expecting, and evidence would seem to point in that direction, then he was grossly mistaken.

Before we proceed further, we should try and formulate a picture of this man, Hippolyte Bouchard, and the revolutionary crew he led to invade the Spanish coastal settlements of California. Bouchard was a Frenchman who became a citizen of Argentina in 1813. He was a sailor and corsair who fought in the service of Argentina, Chile and Peru during the War of Independence against Spain. As for his four-hundred-man crew of "Argentine" revolutionaries—sure, many of his crew were born and raised in Spanish South America, but some of them were also from Great Britain, France, the United States, the Philippines and even the Sandwich Islands (known as Hawaii today). In other words, it is doubtful that, for many of Bouchard's 1818 crew, Argentine independence was much of a motivation. So, what *was* the motivation? Did they want a life of freedom, mayhem and the chance to loot riches? Almost certainly!

By the fall of 1818, Alta California governor Pablo Vicente de Sola received word at his Monterey headquarters that Hippolyte Bouchard and his force of revolutionary pirates were sailing up the coast of Alta California. There was little doubt of Bouchard's destination: Monterey, the Spanish capital of the province. At last, Bouchard's two ships were spotted rounding Point Pinos in late November 1818. Still, Bouchard gave Governor de Sola and the people of Monterey the chance to surrender the town peacefully. The response Bouchard received back was unexpected: not only did Governor de Sola insist that the loyal Spanish subjects of Monterey would *not* surrender, but he also insisted that they would fight to the last man in defense of their city.

Meanwhile, the governor ordered all women, children and elderly to evacuate Monterey and take refuge at a valley rancho (on the outskirts of present-day Salinas). At the same time, any and all able-bodied men and teen boys capable of firing a weapon were herded up to El Castillo to await the arrival of Bouchard's enemy ships in the harbor. A few men and a couple of cannons were stationed about a quarter of a mile below the fort, on a lower point, facing out toward the bay. Altogether, the force perhaps consisted of some thirty men. Nervously, they awaited the arrival of the dreaded Bouchard and his crew of revolutionary pirates.

Later that night, on November 21, 1818, two ships silently glided into view. The larger one, a black ship dubbed the *Argentina*, which was captained by Bouchard himself, came to a stop about two miles offshore. A smaller war ship, the *Santa Rosa*, however, moved close to the shore, coming to a stop in the harbor just below El Castillo. Soon, a voice from the small war ship was heard calling up to the men of El Castillo. The voice was demanding that the Spaniard surrender.

History does not record who fired first, but it was most likely the soldiers of El Castillo. The cannon fight was underway! Certainly, the tiny *Santa Rosa* put up a fierce offense, but by the time it did, the vessel had already been badly damaged, whether the damage was from El Castillo cannon fire or from the onshore battery a bit farther away (but which had the ship easily in their sights). The small Argentine war ship ceased firing and immediately raised the white flag of surrender. It is estimated that about five crewmen of the *Santa Rosa* were killed in the fight. The survivors of the disabled *Santa Rosa* climbed into their lifeboats and rowed out to the safety of the *Argentina*. Then, to the disbelieving eyes of the Monterey defenders, Bouchard's formidable war ship, *Argentina*, sailed away, disappearing from view.

There was singing and celebrating that night at El Castillo. The pirates had been defeated! Apparently, the happy citizens of Monterey did not realize that the true terror was to come the next morning. The pirates would return—and they would come with full force by land!

Yes, though Bouchard's smaller ship, the *Santa Rosa*, had been disabled, Bouchard and his crew, along with the survivors of the *Santa Rosa*, had not sailed for home. Rather, they had simply retreated far enough so as not to be seen by the El Castillo troops. Unbeknownst to the troops, Bouchard and crew laid anchor only a couple of miles down the coast (there is still some debate as to whether Bouchard landed somewhere in the vicinity of today's Hopkins Marine Laboratory in Monterey or in Lover's Point in Pacific Grove). Upon anchorage, Bouchard and some four hundred armed men unloaded half a dozen cannons onto rowboats and rowed ashore. Once on land, Bouchard and his army of pirates marched in the direction of El Castillo.

The soldiers of El Castillo were in for quite a rude awakening the next morning. Upon getting their first view of the four-hundred-man pirate force marching toward them over the grassy hills, the thirty-some defenders of El Castillo—and indeed, of the Alta California capital itself—did what prudent soldiers anywhere would have done: they fled! The pirate revolutionaries soon overran El Castillo, and the multinational force of pirates took possession of any and all arms and ammunition left behind. It was actually two Sandwich Islanders who tore down the El Castillo Spanish flag. Soon, the flag of the United Provinces of the Rio de la Plata flew over El Castillo. Bouchard and his men were hardly finished, however. They had only taken El Castillo, the tiny harbor fort. The main "city," the capital of Spanish California, was still a mile away. They knew that there would almost certainly be a battle for control of the city, but Bouchard, no doubt, was confident that his forces would easily win.

What Bouchard and his men did not realize, however, was that the previous night's cannon fight would be the only armed resistance they would face at Monterey Bay. They marched onto the Presidio of Monterey virtually unopposed, save for a few half-hearted rifle shots from El Castillo, before the Monterey troops fled. The soldiers who had defended El Castillo that morning and the night before had galloped away to safety in the hills or out to the valley. These deserters included Governor Vicente de Sola as well.

The cannon fight between the defenders of El Castillo and the Argentine revolutionary ship in the harbor below marked the most furious pirate attack in California history. In fact, that battle—won by the motley crew of Monterey soldiers (at least for that night)—would also turn out to be the one and only land-to-sea battle in California history!

On one hand, it would seem miraculous that the El Castillo forces were able to defeat one of Bouchard's war ships, though it was a smaller war vessel. On the other hand, to stand on the grassy mound ramparts that now mark the El Castillo site is to gain a clearer perspective. The bay waters are almost right below the El Castillo site. There is only a roadway between the edge of the steep hill and the harbor water. However, in 1818, even that roadway was not there—the water came right up to the cliff below the fort! In other words, the *Santa Rosa* made the mistake of underestimating the firepower of El Castillo by sailing far too close to the El Castillo batteries. Perhaps it was simply a case of overconfidence. Once the war ship was hit by cannon fire, it sustained too much damage in order to back-peddle (so to speak) and retreat quickly. Hence, Bouchard suffered an embarrassing (and somewhat costly) loss of a ship and a few men in that round, but it was only a temporary setback, as the next day's events would prove.

The next day, the Bouchard Attack saga moved to another locale in Monterey: the site of what was once the Presidio of Monterey. However, before I move on from the Lower Presidio Historic Park, why not explore the full gamut of history to be found on this acreage? For instance, human history at the Lower Presidio Historic Park goes back some two thousand years. For most of that time, this hillside overlooking the bay was home to an important California Native American village and, possibly, a significant native trading spot as well. There are Native American rock mortars—used to grind nuts into meal—at the site, as well as a large, ancient Native American

Perched on the hillside between El Castillo and Fort Mervine is this remnant of the centuries-long Indian occupation of this area: the mysterious Indian "Rain Rock." *From author's photo collection.*

ceremonial stone known as the "Indian Rain Rock." Its surface is covered with small circular indentions made by the natives who lived here. As to what these circular indentions indicate, it is thought that they may have recorded child births or the passing of seasons, but no one is sure.

Farther up the hill, behind the "Rain Rock" you can see cannons pointed out over an earthen mound. These mark the spot where U.S. Fort Mervine once stood. This U.S. military outpost was meant to take the place of El Castillo after the United States took control of Monterey in 1846. However, the attacks by land and sea, attacks Fort Mervine was expected to defend against, never materialized. That's because shortly after the United States took possession of Monterey, the town almost immediately lost its former importance. Gold was discovered in the Sierra foothills to the east, and Monterey emptied out almost overnight; almost every able-bodied male headed east in search of gold. Meanwhile, the capital of California moved to San Jose before finally moving to Sacramento to be near the new population center of California. Fort Mervine was soon abandoned and fell into disrepair.

View of San Carlos Church and the old Presidio site from the east side of Lake El Estero. No doubt a few citizens of Monterey who did not flee Bouchard's attack watched the burning from this vantage point. *From author's photo collection.*

A few yards away from the Fort Mervine site there is a large stone monument and eagle statue that stand prominently at the edge of the grassy hillside. That structure is the Sloat Monument, erected in 1896 to mark the momentous occasion when American forces, under the command of Commodore John Sloat, sailed into Monterey Bay, came ashore and hoisted the American flag at the Monterey Custom House. With this raising of the United States flag, California came under American authority for the first time. Down the hill from the Sloat Monument there is the Presidio of Monterey Museum, which is filled with displays covering the site's history, from the days of the Rumsien settlement and the landings of Vizcaíno and Serra to the early twentieth century, when the U.S. Presidio was the training base for the horse-and-rider soldiers of the Eleventh Cavalry.

9

Bouchard Attack on Monterey, Part 2

WHEN: November 1818
WHERE: Site of San Carlos Cathedral and the Royal Presidio (Monterey)

As stated before, the Monterey Presidio of the Spanish-Mexican period was in an altogether different location from today's U.S. Army Presidio and Defense Language Institute at Monterey. The distance between the two Presidios is only about a mile, but while today's Presidio is situated on the hillside overlooking Monterey harbor, the old Presidio was located on the lowlands, next to Lake El Estero.

It's easy to miss the location of the old Monterey Presidio—in fact, innumerable locals and tourists drive right past it on the busy Fremont Street thoroughfare without even realizing they are rolling right past what was once the old Spanish settlement of Monterey. In fact, the formerly walled-in Presidio of Monterey was once the cultural and government epicenter of Spanish and Mexican–era California. Today, once visitors are on the grounds, they can visit the Presidio's old stone church, San Carlos Cathedral, the oldest continuously operating church in California. The church was then known as the Royal Presidio Chapel because the royally appointed governors of Alta California worshipped there. This venerable old church is the only surviving structure of what was once the old Presidio of Monterey. The building's survival is no small feat considering that, in November 1818, Bouchard and his pirates put the Presidio of Monterey to the torch! And by burning down much of the Presidio, Bouchard and his men essentially burned down Monterey itself.

Why should the old Presidio of Monterey be considered the "City" of Monterey back in 1818? Because in 1818, there was no City of Monterey outside the walls of the Presidio. There was not even a small town. There was only a small handful of adobe homes on the mesa hillside, just outside the walls of the Presidio. Inside the walls was the "Governor's Mansion" (actually just a small adobe house), where the governor of Spanish California lived and worked. There were also quarters for the married soldiers and their families, a barracks for single soldiers, a tiny brig, stables, storerooms, workshops and, of course, the Royal Presidio Chapel, which was easily the largest and most impressive structure in 1818 Monterey.

The field that is, today, just across the street from the chapel was, along with a part of the parking lot just beyond it, the center plaza of the old Presidio. It was there that soldiers drilled, children played and Native American and Spanish women worked. Surrounding that center plaza was three hundred square feet of fortress walls with sentry towers. As an interesting historical side note, that grassy recreational field, as nondescript as it appears today, was essentially, for a few months in 1776, the city of San Francisco. I say this because from March to June 1776, the Spanish settlers from Mexico, who were brought up to Alta California by trailblazer Juan Bautista de Anza,

The outside walls of the Monterey Presidio, drawn about ten years after the Bouchard attack. Note that the presidio has been fully rebuilt. *Courtesy of the Mayo Hayes O'Donnell Library.*

A rare eighteenth-century view of the plaza inside Monterey's Spanish Presidio. Note the tiny presidio church, which dates the drawing to pre-1794 (when the great stone Royal Presidio Chapel was built). For some sixty years, this fort, essentially, was Monterey. *Courtesy of the Mayo Hayes O'Donnell Library.*

camped out in the center plaza of the Monterey Presidio. In June 1776, most of those same settlers finally got permission from the governor to ride north and settle what would become the city of San Francisco.

If you recall where we left off in our story about the Bouchard Attack, Bouchard and his men had just overrun the El Castillo fortress, and the Monterey defenders had fled in the face of Bouchard's four-hundred-man pirate force! Upon capturing El Castillo, Bouchard set his sights on the Presidio of Monterey itself—and he expected that the soldiers of El Castillo would take up positions there to defend the Presidio. What the pirates found upon their arrival at the Presidio, however, was a fortress and church (the Royal Presidio Chapel) left completely undefended! The revolutionary pirates did capture one Monterey man, however, a drunk by the name of Molina. He was not a great prize, but as for the Presidio itself, that was a different story!

Remember earlier when I talked about the part of the *Pirates of the Caribbean* ride at Disneyland where the boat passes through a burning Spanish town being ransacked by raucous pirates? That was essentially the scene that took place within the three-hundred-square-foot acreage in front of and around today's San Carlos Cathedral. For a week, and maybe more, Bouchard's pirates had their way with the deserted Presidio. They looted the homes and buildings, grabbing any valuables they could get their hands on, and they no doubt partook of any hard drink left behind. Last but not least, the pirates burned the Presidio almost, but not quite, to the ground. Then, Bouchard and his pirates loaded their ill-gotten bounty onto their ships and sailed away, never to return.

In light of this blatant and seemingly out-of-control pirating behavior, one can only wonder how the Royal Presidio Chapel could still be standing today. Perhaps you're assuming that today's San Carlos Cathedral is a post-1818 reconstruction of the original church, but that is not the case. The church today is the original church that was built in 1794. It has been in continual use (with the exception of a few weeks in 2007, when the church underwent much-needed renovations) since the 1790s. So, just how did the San Carlos Cathedral so thoroughly escape the fate of the rest of the Presidio structures?

Well, as it turns out, Bouchard's men were actually not completely out of his control, even amid that raucous week of burning and looting. Bouchard, being a good Catholic, respected the sanctity of the church. Apparently, Bouchard gave strict orders to his men that the Royal Presidio Chapel was not to be touched. Incredibly, especially given the multi-nationality and multi-religious makeup of his revolutionary mercenaries, his orders were obeyed. Also, amazingly, Bouchard and his men did not hike the relatively short five miles over the hills to Mission San Carlos Borromeo (today known as the Carmel Mission) to ransack the gold and silver valuables—mostly church implements—that they must have known were kept there. Actually, they may not have found much loot, because, upon hearing that Bouchard's ships were on their way to Monterey Bay, it is said that the mission padres had their valuables hidden in a remote canyon in Carmel Valley. They assumed, like the priests of the Royal Presidio Chapel, that Bouchard's pirates would loot and destroy the church, but that did not happen.

The governor, soldiers and civilians of Monterey returned after Bouchard and his pirates were safely gone. The Monterey Presidio was rebuilt and re-fortified, and life went on in Spanish Monterey as before—at least until 1822, when Monterey underwent a peaceful transition to become the Mexican capital of Alta California.

To conclude the story of Hippolyte Bouchard and his 1818 "pirate" attack on Monterey, it must be remembered that Bouchard is not

This is a 1913 photograph of the church at Mission San Carlos Borromeo (Carmel Mission). Like the Royal Presidio Chapel in Monterey, this sacred church (and its valuables) was left untouched by Bouchard and his men in 1818. *Courtesy of the Library of Congress Prints and Photographs Division.*

considered a "pirate" by everyone. In fact, to the people of Argentina, Chile and Peru, Bouchard is simply considered a revolutionary—even a hero. To the people of South America, Bouchard is no more a vagabond than the revolutionaries who fought against the British for liberty from 1775 to 1781 are to the people of the United States. The citizens of Monterey, however, especially those of old, absolutely did consider Bouchard to be a pirate, especially in light of his attack and the looting and burning that followed. On the other hand, not a single citizen of Monterey lost their life in that 1818 attack, but it can also be said that none of them stuck around long enough to be victimized by Bouchard's fighters. So, by one definition, Bouchard was not a pirate, but by another, he absolutely was. In the end, each person is welcome to make up his or her own mind on the matter.

At the site of the old Monterey Presidio, it's worth one's while to do more than just gaze at the surroundings and imagine the fiery chaos that took place there. Visitors should explore the church itself, but they should be mindful that it is still an active place of worship. They should also know that the San Carlos Cathedral, in addition to witnessing and surviving the Bouchard pirate invasion, is (again) the oldest continuously-in-use church in California, the oldest structure in Monterey, the first stone church in California, the first architecturally designed structure in California and the first church in California to be designated a cathedral. Visitors should also go to the Heritage Center Museum next door to the San Carlos Cathedral. There, one can find not only Spanish- and Mexican-period presidio artifacts and signage communicating the rich history of the Presidio, but they can also see a chunk of the venerated Vizcaíno-Serra Oak!

Visitors should also be aware that, while the San Carlos Cathedral is the only standing structure that is left from the days of the old Presidio, the church is not the only remnant of the old fort. Across the grassy recreational field is a corner fence separating the field from the old YMCA building. On the other side of the fence, one can see a metal awning overhanging a slope of dirt—beneath that awning is what appears to be rock rubble, but it is actually the stone footings of the Presidio wall, which is all that remains above ground. It may not look like much, but it is a rare remnant of the Spanish-period Presidio. Indeed, these aged stone footings would have incredible stories to tell of early California history—including the terrifying invasion of Bouchard's pirates—if only they could speak!

There is a reason as to *why* there is virtually nothing left of the old Presidio, even the structures rebuilt right after the 1818 attack. By the 1830s, the Presidio fortress was fast becoming obsolete. The War of Independence against Spain was over, so there was no imminent threat of Latin American revolutionaries attacking the city. Most of all, however, the town of Monterey was now growing outside the walls of the Presidio. In fact, the town was moving pointedly in the direction of today's Fisherman's Wharf. Monterey, at the time, was under Mexican rule, and the biggest change of that transition was that California became

Above and opposite: Different views of San Carlos Cathedral, formerly known as the Royal Presidio Chapel. Miraculously, this historic church (built in 1794) was not harmed when Bouchard's "pirates" burned and ransacked the surrounding Presidio in 1818. *From author's photo collection.*

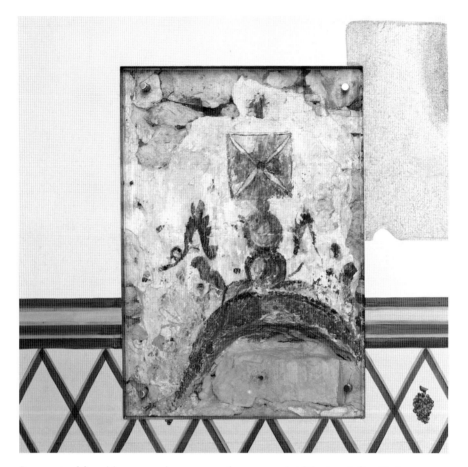

Remnants of Spanish-era murals were recently uncovered at Monterey's San Carlos Cathedral. This wall art was probably visible in 1818, when Bouchard and his men burned the buildings around the church. *Photograph by Carol Highsmith, courtesy of the Library of Congress Prints and Photographs Division.*

open to foreign trade. Commerce was booming and the "action" began revolving around the Monterey waterfront, especially considering that was where the Custom House was located. The Custom House, built in 1827, was the primary port of entry for all goods entering California via foreign (primarily British and American) trade ships. Also, by the 1830s, more and more of the Mexican governors of Alta California chose not to live inside the old Presidio—or in some cases, not even in Monterey at all.

Later, in the 1840s, a new military headquarters, El Cuartel, was constructed outside the walls of the Presidio. The old Spanish-era fort

Artist depiction of Monterey some twenty years after the 1818 Bouchard attack. Note that, by the time these depictions were made, the town had grown outside the Presidio walls and stretched toward the waterfront. *Lithograph by W.M. Endicott after sketch by J.W. Revere, courtesy of Library of Congress Prints and Photographs Division.*

Another depiction of early Monterey in the years following the 1818 attack. *Artists: Jose Dorio Arquello and Thomas O. Larkin. Courtesy of the Library of Congress Prints and Photographs Division, Historic American Buildings Survey.*

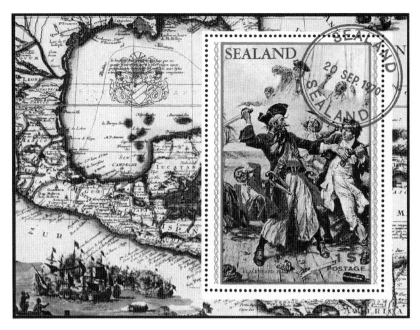

Map of the Caribbean and Central America, along with a stamp depicting the terrifying Captain Blackbeard (killed in 1718 off the coast of North Carolina) in battle. *Courtesy of Adobestock.com.*

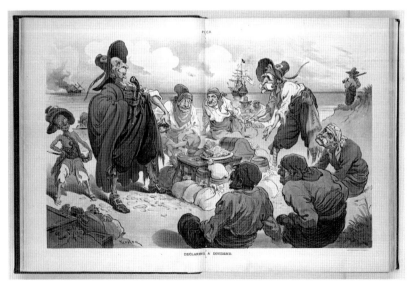

Pirates gathered around a treasure chest on the beach—this is actually a satirical United States political cartoon from 1906. *Artist: Udo J. Keppler. Courtesy of the Library of Congress Prints and Photographs Division.*

had outlived its usefulness, and with the governors and soldiers no longer making use of it, the Presidio was gradually abandoned. The walls surrounding the plaza, the quarters workshops and the storerooms fell into disrepair. Eventually, Monterey residents building homes outside the Presidio simply helped themselves to the stones, roof tiles and adobe materials that made up the walls and structure of the Presidio. These materials were spirited away for use in the construction or expansion of new homes and business buildings. By the late 1800s, most of the old Presidio of Monterey had disappeared from view.

Epilogue

irates, especially the fearsome characters from the peak of the Age of Pirates (1650–1720), seem so fanciful that, at times, it's hard to tell which pirates are fictional and which are not. For instance, consider the following list of rogue pirates: Captain Hook, Black Bart, Jack Sparrow, Long John Silver and Blackbeard. Which of those five are fictional and which are nonfictional? Answer: Blackbeard and Black Bart were not figures of fiction—they were actual living, breathing people. The point of this is: the life, times, exploits and even the over-the-top physical appearance of pirates from that era seem like the figment of a novelist's (like Robert Louis Stevenson's) imagination as opposed to actual chapters from human history. Perhaps that's why pirates continue to loom large in the imaginations of people—especially young people.

In light of the continuing popularity of pirates and the pirate era, a natural question arises, especially from the point of view of concerned parents: should these admittedly violent sea robbers be celebrated, glorified and romanticized? If we're talking about a literal definition of "celebrating," "glorifying" and "romanticizing," then the answer should be no. Wanton violence and robbery, unhealthy (and, at times, brutal) womanizing and drunken carousing are hardly behavior traits to celebrate and glorify. We certainly do not want young people to emulate such behavior. The fact remains, however, that more of us would rather hop aboard the *Pirates of the Caribbean* ride at Disneyland than turn away in revulsion. Is that an indictment on our society that we are guilty of celebrating and glorifying pirate era mayhem? I don't think so.

I contend that to "celebrate" or "glorify" a behavior is to imply consent—even enjoyment—of deplorable actions. Would any of us think well of pirates if we were their victims on the high seas or the streets of a Spanish harbor town? Would we ask the authorities to overlook their acts of murder or general terrorization of innocent citizens? Would we cheer at seeing them stagger drunk along the streets and piers of port towns, wreaking havoc on the general peace? If you're someone of that kind of sociopathic bent, perhaps you would—as for the rest of us, definitely not.

To bring the issue closer to home for those of us who live in the twenty-first century: is a fascination with the pirates of old the same as having an unhealthy fascination with the activities of today's street gangs, who are also known for their penchant for violence and mayhem? I would say there is a distinct difference, and it has to do with a T+T (Tragedy plus Time) equation. The phenomenon of the T+T equation (if you don't know what that is, you should check out the Woody Allen movie *Crimes and Misdemeanors*, where the the concept is explained in hilarious manner by the pretentious Alan Alda character) is basically that tragic and terrible history is made far more palatable when one is separated from it by the cushion of several decades (at least) or, better yet, centuries. For example, it's T+T that allows millions of visitors to stomach a visit to the ruins of the Coliseum at Rome, despite the carnage that took place there. We simply would not be able to function as human beings if we internalized every human act of cruelty and inhumanity that has ever happened, so we shake our heads, agree that great tragedies took place at the Coliseum and proceed to pose and take pictures. Now, we can see the acts of cruelty and violence against fellow human on the news or read about in the newspaper—*those* truly upset and anger us (at least I hope they do) because the tragedy is immediate, the victims are suffering as we speak and the monsters who perpetrated the violence are, oftentimes, still walking among us. Yes, folks, there is a difference, so, for better or worse, T+T is a very real phenomenon.

I will submit that, at the very least, unlike the despicable street gangs of today, the pirates of old had certifiable skills (they were expert sailors) *and* they were held to a Code of Honor, though it was, admittedly, a warped code that would hardly stand up to our Constitution. Still, I would submit that even the *concept* of a "Code of Honor" is completely alien to today's mindless criminal element. Suffice it to say, pirates—for better or worse—still have our undivided attention. We read pirate books. We go to pirate movies. We step onto pirate rides at amusement parks. We even dress up as pirates for Halloween, buy pirate souvenirs at gift shops and, yes, some of us enjoy growling, "Yaaaarrrrrrrrrgh," or "Avast, matey!" for the amusement of our friends.

I will also assert that there is a difference between a fascination with pirates and a genuine glorification and celebration of their actions. The Age of Pirates is long past. Though there are modern-day pirates, they no longer prowl the waters in quaint wooden sailing ships. You won't find a pirate captain wearing a long coat and a striking wig of cascading woolen hair that flows from beneath a distinctive tricorn hat. Pirates no longer toss huge, crudely struck silver and gold coins into heavy wooden chests with ornate brass trims. Pirates no longer take over port towns in the Caribbean, carouse in the street, fire pistols into the air and sing loud sea chanteys as they swig down bottles of rum. You get the point: they are long gone, so it is now safe and palatable to confront them.

I can tell you this. My interest in pirates was piqued not only by my love of the Peter Pan story (I was familiar with the story record before I was familiar with the Disney movie) but also by the *Pirates of the Caribbean* ride at Disneyland. When I was little, that ride terrified me—but later, in my teens, I was fascinated by the sense that the ride was taking me back to an intriguing place and time that was long gone. Because I also happened to be a coin collector, that Disney ride also prompted this thought: *I have to own a coin from the time of pirates!* A few months later, I finally bought one, a French copper coin from the 1640s. Since then, I have been fortunate enough to amass a collection of pirate-era coins, as well as other small artifacts from that period.

My interest in pirates also encouraged me to learn more about the wider period of history of which the Age of Pirates was just a part. It was a time known today as the Age of Exploration and Settlement, though it could also correctly be classified as the Early American Colonial period. My fascination ultimately led me to a master's degree in American history, and it all started because a Disney boat ride through scenes of early eighteenth-century pirate activity, complete with pirates, pirate ships and pirate treasure caves made me feel like I had been transported back to an altogether different time and place.

I suppose the debate over whether a fascination with the Age of Pirates is healthy or unhealthy will never end. Even so, whether or not you believe such an interest to be healthy or unhealthy (especially for young people), I submit that such an interest in this period of history can actually evolve into an undeniably healthy interest in early Colonial history—or better yet, history in general.

The great thing about history is that, in one sense, it is indeed all in the past. "Done and in the books," as they say. Then again, it isn't really. History is constantly evolving. That's not to say that the events of the past are changing but that our understanding of them is constantly evolving. New discoveries are constantly coming to light. For instance, archaeologists are continually making new discoveries at the site of Jamestown, our nation's first permanent British settlement. Newly recovered artifacts at the Jamestown site are forcing historians to reevaluate long-held assumptions about the first Jamestown settlers (for example, ground finds show that the early Jamestown settlers were hardly as "lazy" as earlier believed and that they were actually far more enterprising than previously thought by American historians). In fact, it was long assumed by historians that we would never uncover the remains of the earliest Jamestown fort, because it was believed that the James River had swallowed up the site. Digs next to the James River in the mid-1990s completely disproved that assumption. The original fort site is indeed above ground, and it can be visited today.

By the same token, new archaeological findings are adding to our nation's pirate history as well. In just the last few years, the long-lost remains of Blackbeard's flagship, the *Queen Anne's Revenge*, have been discovered off the waters of North Carolina. Once the artifacts are fully brought ashore and studied by scientists, we will have new information about what life was like on a real pirate ship. Perhaps we will learn something new about Blackbeard the pirate himself.

I don't believe this humble book will be the last word on Monterey Bay pirate history. My hunch is that new discoveries will be found in the waters or sands of the Monterey Peninsula—discoveries that will further tie this little corner of California to pirate history. Until such new "pirate" discoveries come to light, consider this guidebook just the beginning.

A Self-Guided
Monterey Bay Pirate Tour

I t's absolutely possible to hit every Monterey Peninsula pirate history site discussed in this guidebook in one excursion. I would not recommend it, however, unless you're really in a hurry and your motivation is just to say, "I've been there." For instance, a site like Point Lobos State Park *demands* that you linger more than just a few minutes, which is why I recommend making at least two separate excursions and why I divided the various Monterey Bay pirate history tours that follow. In fact, you might even wish to make *three* separate excursions, making the two Pebble Beach pirate history sites part of one big Pebble Beach and Seventeen Mile Drive trip.

Nevertheless, I divided the major pirate history excursion into two trips. The first covers the sites at Monterey, Pacific Grove and Pebble Beach. The second excursion takes you to the two Carmel sites. As mentioned earlier in the guidebook, the route I lay out will not take you to the pirate history sites in chronological order since they are, instead, placed in a spatially linear order, more or less.

EXCURSION 1
MONTEREY, PACIFIC GROVE AND PEBBLE BEACH

SITE 1: SAN CARLOS CATHEDRAL
The cathedral is located at 500 Church Street (see chapter "Bouchard Attack on Monterey, Part II"). After taking in the rich history (both pirate and non-

pirate related history), the next stop is quite close by. In fact, it's just a few blocks away.

Site 2: Robert Louis Stevenson House

The Robert Louis Stevenson House is located down the street from the cathedral at 530 Houston Street (see chapter "*Treasure Island* and the Monterey Peninsula"). This is where you can commune with the ghosts of the old inn, one of whom may be that of Robert Louis Stevenson himself. But, if you'd rather not dwell on that kind of spooky scenario, just know you are moving about a place where Stevenson may have already been mentally planning his future pirate novel, *Treasure Island*.

The next stop will require a bit more of driving through town, but it is not a great distance—perhaps a mile or so. Once you cross through downtown Monterey, you will soon arrive at the Pacific Street gate to the Lower Presidio Historic Park. Once you park and are out on foot, walk back in the direction of the white post gate entrance through which you entered. Head all the way down the sidewalk, along Artillery Street, and exit through the gate, where you will arrive at our next location.

Site 3: Vizcaíno-Serra Landing Site

(See chapter on Vizcaíno and the 1602 landing.) After visiting the Vizcaíno-Serra Landing Site, hike back into the Lower Presidio Historic Park, past where you parked your car and out onto the grassy area overlooking Fishermen's Wharf and Monterey harbor. Keep angling left toward the edge of the grassy knoll, and you will eventually see a grassy mound at the edge of the hill, which is our next site.

Site 4: The Old El Castillo Fort Site

(See chapter "Bouchard Attack on Monterey, Part I.") After a morning of taking in four pirate history sites, you may elect to have a casual picnic lunch on the grounds of the Lower Presidio Historic Park (there are even picnic benches next to the Presidio Museum).

Upon leaving Monterey Lower Presidio Historic Park, you will head in the direction of Cannery Row, but you should continue past that fascinating (and quite historical in its own right) avenue, following the road that winds south along the picturesque coastline of Pacific Grove. Eventually, you will arrive at the next stop on our Monterey Bay pirate history tour.

Site 5: Point Pinos

(See chapter "Juan Rodriguez Cabrillo, First New World Pirate.") If you recall, this is the first Monterey Bay shoreline spotted and charted by explorer Juan Cabrillo in 1542. Point Pinos is also the farthest point that the Peninsula juts out into the Pacific, thus making for some truly dramatic surf crashing on the rocks.

After exploring and pondering the mysteries of Point Pinos, return to your car and continue along Sunset Boulevard, past some of the loveliest and most dramatic shoreline you will ever see. After a couple of miles or so, the road will eventually turn uphill and away from the ocean. Soon, you will come to the intersection of Sunset and Seventeen Mile Drive. Turn right, pay your entrance fee at the gate and head inside. After passing the Spanish Bay Inn and Resort on your right, follow the Seventeen-Mile Drive signs as you head toward the ocean. The first beach you come to is our next stop.

Site 6: Moss Beach

(See chapter on Sir Francis Drake and a possible Pebble Beach landing.) Remember, however, that there are two sites where the Sir Francis Drake–era artifacts were said to have been discovered—one was at Moss Beach and the other was at Fanshell Beach. So, after visiting Moss Beach, you will also want to drive another four miles south to our next location.

Site 7: Fanshell Beach

(See chapter on Sir Francis Drake and a possible Pebble Beach landing.) Your stop at Fanshell Beach will complete the first excursion of your self-guided Monterey Bay pirate history tour. Congratulate yourself on this achievement and enjoy the rest of your day by continuing along the rest of the ultra-scenic Seventeen-Mile Drive.

EXCURSION 2
CARMEL AND JUST SOUTH OF CARMEL

There are only two Monterey Peninsula pirate history sites to visit on today's excursion, but each site is so jaw-droppingly beautiful (in addition to being hugely historically significant) that you will probably want to take your time at each locale to take it all in.

Assuming you are making your approach from the direction of Monterey, you will simply head south on Highway 1–South. On this drive, you will ascend Carmel Hill before the highway descends for about a two-mile stretch until you reach the bottom of the hill. There, you will pass the Rio Road intersection (take note of that road, because you will turn there on the way back), continuing your trek due south on Highway 1.

Just past Rio Road, you'll notice that you're leaving "civilization" behind and entering the "wild" coast (hills, trees, pastureland and beaches with no paved parking lots). About three miles past the last lighted intersection, you will come to a stretch of pine forest along Highway 1—at this point, keep an eye out for the sign to Point Lobos State Natural Preserve.

Site 1: Point Lobos

(See chapter "*Treasure Island* and the Monterey Peninsula.") I recommend starting your main Point Lobos jaunt at Whaler's Cove—and if there truly ever was genuine, nonfiction pirate history at Point Lobos, my money says Whaler's Cove was where it took place. From Whaler's Cove, hike along the hilly, forested trails that meander along what was almost certainly the landscape that inspired the novel *Treasure Island*.

Tired as you may be from your Point Lobos hike—and you may find it hard to pry yourself away from this gem of a nature preserve—save up just a little energy for your last Monterey Peninsula pirate history stop.

For the journey to our next location, return back to Highway 1, in the direction of Carmel. After about three miles, you will again come to the intersection of Rio Road. There, turn left and follow the road as it takes you through a residential neighborhood and finally past the front of the historical Carmel Mission (most definitely worth a visit, though not part of our tour). At the corner of the Carmel Mission, turn left onto Lasuen Drive, then follow that road as it winds—and I mean *really* winds—around the side and back of the Carmel Mission until you arrive at the entrance to the Mission Ranch Hotel. This rustic hotel, once a working ranch, is an ideal place to stop and look out at picturesque Carmel Bay. In fact, you can see your final destination in the distance from this location. Still, you will need to eventually leave Mission Ranch and continue toward Carmelo Street for about a mile until you arrive at our next site.

Site 2: Carmel River State Beach

(See chapter "A Carmel Bay Pirate Shipwreck?") Here, you can park the car and walk out onto the white-sand beach near the place where the river and ocean meet (or almost meet, depending on the time of year). While here, ponder the possible pirate shipwreck that might have taken place here, as well as the suffering of the 1769 Gaspar de Portola expedition that encamped here that chilling December in 1769 while on their quest to finally settle Spanish California!

There is no need to rush at this site because you have completed your self-guided Monterey Peninsula pirate history tour! Congratulations!

Bibliography

Books

Bolton, Herbert Eugene, ed. *Fray Juan Crespi: Missionary Explorer on the Pacific Coast 1769–1774*. Berkeley: University of California Press, 1927.

Cook, Todd. *Nueva California*. Vols. I and II. Moorpark, CA: Floricanto Press, 2018.

Fink, Augusta. *Monterey County: The Dramatic Story of Its Past*. Santa Cruz, CA: Western Tanager Press, 1972.

Kelsey, Harry. *Sir Francis Drake: The Queen's Pirate*. New Haven, CT: Yale University Press, 1998.

Reinstedt, Randall A. *More Than Memories: History & Happenings of the Monterey Peninsula*. Monterey, CA: Monterey Peninsula Chamber of Commerce Foundation, 1985.

———. *Tales Treasures and Pirates of Old Monterey*. Carmel, CA: Ghost Town Publications, 1976.

Uhrowoczik, Peter. *The Burning of Monterey: The 1818 Attack on California by the Privateer Bouchard*. N.p.: Cyril Books, 2001.

Magazine Articles:

Goddio, Frank. "San Diego: An Account of Adventure, Deceit and Intrigue." *National Geographic Magazine* (July 1994).

Lyon, Eugene. "Track of the Manila Galleons." *National Geographic Magazine* (September 1990).

Websites

Breschini, Gary S. "Coastal Navigation and Exploration of the Monterey Bay Area." Monterey County Historical Society. www.mchsmuseum.com.
———. "Sebastian Vizcaíno's Exploration of Monterey in 1602–1603." Monterey County Historical Society. www.mchsmuseum.com.

About the Author

Todd Cook is a writer and historian who has lived on the Monterey Peninsula for over twenty-five years. An avid numismatist, Todd has written five articles for *COINS* magazine from 1990 to 2006. His published books include the historical novels, *Madame* (2011), *The Bleeding Door* (2015) and *Nueva California* (2018), as well as the nonfiction book *Uncovered: The Lost Coins of Early America* (2006). In addition to writing these books, Todd helped identify and catalogue several early California artifacts in his work with the Carmel Mission Arts and Artifact Inventory Team.

Visit us at
www.historypress.com